LEONARDO
THE ULTIMATE SECRET

ISBN: 9798671509434

© 1996-2020 Giovanni Pala
Management:
Barbara Harris
aphousela@yahoo.com

First Edition: December 2020

© 2020 ALIC Publishing House Inc.
2399 North Sepulveda Blvd.
Los Angeles, California 90077
U.S.A

© All rights reserved worldwide. This Book, the text, the images cannot be reproduced in any form without the written authorization of the author. Any public display is also strictly proibited.

The draws and the original three-dimensional images and picture, copyrights by © Giovanni Pala, 1996-2020.

It is forbidden the copy this book. Distributing pirate copies of this book, may result in criminal sanctions including fines and imprisonment and/or civil actions a the payment of damages. This Book are protected by International copy-rights.

Cover Design by: Thomas Bennett | Eduard Hill | Steven Harris |

Internet: www.giovannipalawriter.com

GIOVANNI PALA

LEONARDO
THE ULTIMATE SECRET

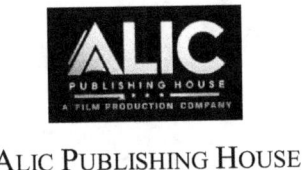

Alic Publishing House

*"The poet ranks far below the painter
in the rapresentation of visible things,
and far below the musician
in that of invisible things."*

Leonardo da Vinci

Introduction

What you are about to read is the story of a little-known side of Leonardo da Vinci, the story of his relationship with music and the extraordinary 'secret code' he concealed in his celebrated painting *The Last Supper*. We will alternate chapters on his life with interludes describing the stages in my long research; doubts, second thoughts, errors, intuitions and solutions are recorded here in the order in which they occurred. As well as gathering together the little we know about da Vinci the musician, this book also provides a revolutionary interpretation of the famous fresco, laden with hidden meanings which until now had not even been suspected.

In this painting Leonardo da Vinci used not only the language of painting, but also the languages of music, creating a harmonious whole composed of various dimensions and levels of understanding. It is as if he had created a multimedia work of art centuries before the computer was invented, projecting his genius beyond the confines of the time in which he lived, so that his work seems cutting edge even now.

In much of his writing, he predicted events we are now experiencing; from various forms of modern technology (think only of his sketches of embryonic submarines, helicopters and tanks) to the slow and progressive destruction of our world by our own hands.

What I shall reveal as being contained within *The Last Supper* – 'Musical Phrases' – were a mystery not easily solved. I had to look beyond the mural, overcoming the confines of mere visual representation to reach the universe of signs and symbols that Leonardo had hidden within it.

There is no doubt that the mental processes involved in creating works of art are similar to those of discovering scientific truths. Human creativity is expressed through moments of synthesis, inspiration, if you prefer, that are almost the same in all fields. A painter's ability to juxtapose tones of color and that of a musician to juxtapose tones of music are examples of the same kind of intellectual activity. The painter and the musician are both creating new harmonious sequences.

So it is not difficult to imagine that Leonardo, 'an excellent lyre player' according to his contemporaries, could also have a talent for composing music.

On this premise, it is not impossible, as we shall see later, that he might have inserted musical notes into his paintings, even if, being a lover of enigma, he chose not to make it clear that those signs were musical notation. Among the many examples of codes and puzzles that have been concealed deliberately in works of art over the centuries, there are plenty of a musical nature: in the east frieze of the Parthenon (of which fragments have been recomposed and preserved at the British Museum in London), a number of scholars have noted that the figures appear to follow each other both over time and space. The figures are distributed over the frieze at times in tight groups, at others in wider groups, separated from each other. In fact, they appear to be measuring out a rhythm, and again; in Raphael's famous painting *The School of Athens*, one of Pythagoras' young pupils is depicted with a harmonic table in his hands.

In contrast to the research often carried out on Leonardo's works using modern technology (optical and computerized devices, etc.), my research is based on a simple observation of the work that speaks for itself, adding nothing.

The revelation of the 'secret code' is linked to continuous references to *Holy Scripture*, especially to the symbols and images contained in the *Gospels* and, above all, in the *Gospel* according to the Apostle who was closest to Jesus - St. John.

The Last Supper by Leonardo da Vinci is perhaps the most important representation of the times of St. John's *Gospel*; it is like a great sea, in which millions of human eyes and minds have been immersed over the centuries and will certainly continue to be so. But into this great ocean the artist has thrown a message in a bottle, perhaps in the hope that someone, sometime, will find it.

Until now, we have only *looked* at *The Last Supper*; now we are going to *listen* to it, to feed on a life-giving sap that runs anew through this limitless masterpiece.

This research has also given rise to knowledge of what I believe to be the true Leonardo – an artist who acknowledged the existence of a God who is perfection in all its manifestations. He himself stated that painting was directly linked to God, because it shared the same creative force and that music, no less, was capable of representing the invisible.

I owe particular thanks to my wife Carla, who believed in the project and has followed the whole adventure step by step. In addition, I would also like to express my gratitude to my agent Fabio Savoia, Blanca Luisa Jimenèz Covelli, Graeme and Anna Goodwin, Lourdes Covelli, Genaro R. Vavuris, Rosamaria Romo; Giovanni Muscas and his wife, Don Uccio Spanu, Francesco Squintu, Marco Fadda, Saturnino and Giada; my publisher, Steven Harris and the Alic Publishing House who shepherded all the parts of the project to completion.

Finally, my heartfelt appreciation to my parents, other members of my family, and my friends, who always stood by me when the going was tough.

This book is dedicated to my mother Petronilla.

Giovanni Pala

I

Before recounting how I discovered one of the last secrets of the great artist Leonardo da Vinci, I would like to mention an apparently insignificant detail which will, however, play an important role in the story, just as certain tiny details in life, even if we usually perceive them with the benefit of hindsight, are sometimes premonitions of our 'fate'.

I always remember that I studied the works of Leonardo at high school. One day the picture of *The Last Supper* was projected onto the screen and there followed a typical boring lesson on technique, dimensions, perspective – in brief, all the usual things that are learned at school. I interrupted the teacher by raising my hand and asked why the tablecloth showed a series of perfectly vertical and horizontal creases, almost starched in, as if the cloth had been consciously folded and then reopened and placed on the table, and whether the artist had done this in order to refer to something that went beyond the image itself.

The teacher hesitated for a moment to consider the question, then asked me not to interrupt the lesson with such fantasies.

The tablecloth was as she could see it and that was all!

But questions are never asked simply by chance.

A spark that could create a new hypothesis should never be ignored, or worse still, be extinguished. Many years later, while I was studying Leonardo, a my dear friend – who in the meantime had become a painter – was commissioned to make a copy of *The Last Supper* on canvas, obviously using smaller dimensions, to adorn the drawing room of a private house. I was curious to see the technique that my friend used to divide up the large canvas into a serious of squares, after doing the same on the photograph of the original, so that the figures could be enlarged in a perfectly proportionate manner. He did the painting in oils and nuance by nuance those faces and expressions seemed to come back to life. Sometimes, when he wasn't there, I would go to the painting, lift the sheet covering the canvas and observe it in all its most minute details, until it was finally delivered to its new owner.

I had already glimpsed what was hidden there, but did not wish to speak about it until I was sure.

The universal fame of *The Last Supper* is due not only to its unquestionable artistic value, but also to the numerous hypotheses on the mysteries and secret messages that could be concealed within it: from the strangely feminine appearance of the St. John the Apostle (remember *The Da Vinci Code*?) to the absence of the chalice of the Eucharist on the table, the mysterious hand holding a knife seemingly belonging to no-one, and the gestures of some of the Apostles. Some of these 'oddities' have in the past been interpreted as signs of the artist's possible heretical thinking, while others appear to derive directly from his, shall we say 'whimsical' genius.

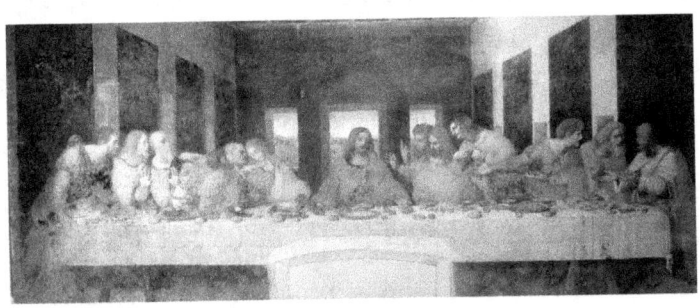

We know from various sources, for example, how much Leonardo, an ironic and provocative inventor and scientist, loved creating puzzles, using mirror writing and generally testing the abilities of his companions. His taste for enigma has often encouraged people to identify in his paintings ideas and subjects that are different from those usually encountered in the History of Art.

I was spurred on by the idea that he had inserted a 'secret code' in *The Last Supper* and left it to posterity as an unavowed legacy. After all, with a manifold genius like his, which excelled in all fields of human knowledge, constrained by fate to live in an historical period where the Catholic Church showed some of its darkest sides, could, in my opinion, perfectly well have entrusted to the knowing work of his brush the task of concealing among colors, light and shade, a secret code that revealed his true way of thinking.

The more I came to know him, the more the idea seemed plausible.

I am now a musicologist and my academic studies mainly concern Renaissance music, so on one hand, approaching the greatest genius of the Italian Renaissance in order to try to understand his mind and most profound vision came naturally to me; on the other hand, I was frustrated by the scarcity of documents relating to Leonardo the musician, whom I *knew* to be the great painter, sculptor, poet and scientist. It is true that among the immense but fragmentary corpus of his handwritten papers, there were some where he had noted down phrases of music, and two or three of his biographers and contemporaries spoke, as we shall see, of his talent as a singer and lyre player, but no-one has ever found a piece of music *written* by Leonardo. Unfortunately, his inestimable gift for creating harmonious wholes, even if it manifested itself in musical form for those listening, was never transcribed in a way that could reach us.

Another reason for this is that in Leonardo's day written music, as we noted in the first chapter, was not yet a widespread phenomenon. Scores existed, of course, but it was above all French and Flemish monks who produced them, so that the few complete works from the late fifteenth century that have survived are those of Johannes Ockeghem, Jacob Obrecht and other minor musicians, and are all complex works of polyphonic sacred music, certainly not music to entertain at court festivities, even if the latter, despite using a relatively restricted range of instruments, was played everywhere. It was only in the fifteen hundreds, in fact, the century of Giovanni Palestrina and Claudio Monteverdi, that Opera and, a little later, Baroque music were born. Mainly thanks to the appearance of a whole series of new instruments which technology made possible towards the middle of the century. Indeed, some scholars maintain that it was precisely Leonardo who made a crucial contribution to the evolution that transformed the *vielle* of the fifteenth century into the viola of the late sixteenth century, showing once again that he was ahead of his contemporaries by generations.

However, let us return to my speculations.

Without a shadow of doubt, the historic and technical assumptions existed to put Leonardo in a position to insert a complete piece of music into *The Last Supper*. From his writings we learn that his concept of painting was that all knowledge had to flow into it, forming a whole which was organic and indeed harmonious. This should not surprise us since, at that time, the step from harmony in the figurative arts to the harmonies of music was smaller than we could imagine today.

In much medieval sacred architecture, for example, the proportion of the figurative elements, the alternation of areas of light and shade or the recurrence of certain decorations, were devised on the basis of a *Perfect Measure* expressed in geometric formulae, the same as those that governed the theory of St. Augustine's treatise *On Music*.

Some scholars had already considered *The Last Supper* from the angle of its 'musicality' and the harmony expressed by its pictorial composition, but they considered it for the most part in a lateral sense.

Having decided to find evidence for my theory of music concealed in the fresco, my investigation into the da Vinci painting began as a kind of personal challenge to its genius, a challenge that over time would cause me to become ever more involved, like a bloodhound following the tracks to a secret that is fascinating to the point of obsession. Obviously, the fact that Leonardo would have known how to play and understand music was not in itself a determining factor. It was a necessary condition, but not sufficient to maintain that the artist had inserted a musical code into the painting. If he had done so, the music would certainly be present in complex and hidden forms, masked in accordance with the typical methods of enigma.

At times, however, an enigma also conceals itself.

At the beginning, I could not even be sure that there really was a mystery, or, at least, that there was one where I thought I would find it.

By its very nature, a secret message must pass unobserved, visible only to the distinguished few who are capable of seeing it.

In my case, apart from a suspicion fed by history and my own personal 'feeling', the conviction that music was hidden somewhere in *The Last Supper* also came from my friend's work as a painter, as he often hid small clues in his canvases instead of signing them with his name or, if he signed them, he did so using a pseudonym.

In the end, I decided that the only way to bring the enigma to light was to look at the painting as if seeing it for the first time, in order to escape the conditioning and customary thinking that often cause us to draw hurried conclusions, especially when it is a work that is universally known, reproduced and incessantly studied.

My observation, however, no matter how neutral and free of any kind of prejudice, needed to be guided by certain questions; in short, I needed to know what I should 'ask' the painting.

The idea of asking questions of a mute painting could seem absurd, and what could I possibly have asked a work that had defied fate, surviving wars, sieges and bombings, that in the past five hundred years had not already received an answer?

Deep inside myself, I felt that the answer had to arise spontaneously from the painting, that Leonardo's work had to speak for itself – indeed, it had to 'play' for itself. I was sure of one thing; if there really was music in it, it could only be dramatic.

How could music not be dramatic if it accompanied the announcement of Christ's passion?

If Leonardo had inserted a musical composition into the representation of such an intense and painful moment in the life of Jesus, it had to be music that was at once sad and solemn.

To find traces of it, I needed to think and use my imagination, no matter how ambitious this may have seemed. In the same way as the painting's creator, to feel I was truly in touch with his intentions, I knew this could only happen if I looked at the original and not at a copy.

So I went regularly to the refectory of Santa Maria delle Grazie in Milan, where *The Last Supper* is to be found. In order to grasp what could be hidden in it.

I needed to look at it from a distance, seeing it in its totality.

From close up I would have risked not seeing those things that had breath, an extension that covered the whole scene.

I do not truly believe in the existence of chance.

Once, in a book by the Jungian psychologist James Hillman, I read that a 'daemon' can act in each of us. This daemon is not seen as an evil presence, but as a personal guide 'allocated to us' by the collective unconscious.

Daemon is a Greek word that the ancients, like Jung, used to define the spirit, the essence of a person. It is the daemon that keeps our memories from before we were born, or from previous lives. The daemon is the bearer of our fate, our secret travelling companion. According to Hillman, this spirit guide, which is the manifestation of our true nature, can come to the surface at any time, like a calling, a vocation or a revelation.

And that is how it happened to me.

One day, my daemon drew my attention to a detail that I already felt was the turnkey of the mystery, the same one I had noted while my friend was creating her copy of *The Last Supper*: my eye was drawn instinctively to the vertical and horizontal lines that creased the tablecloth of the *Holy Table*. Those lines, I had already said to myself, could form a sort of musical outline, compatible with the idea of a stave. For a musician it comes naturally to read any 'grid' as a possible score, just as it comes naturally to them to imagine any musical notation, either of a line of melody or the harmonic structure of a piece, as being transcribed on a base, that is to say on a musical score, which in this case, could be represented by the tablecloth.

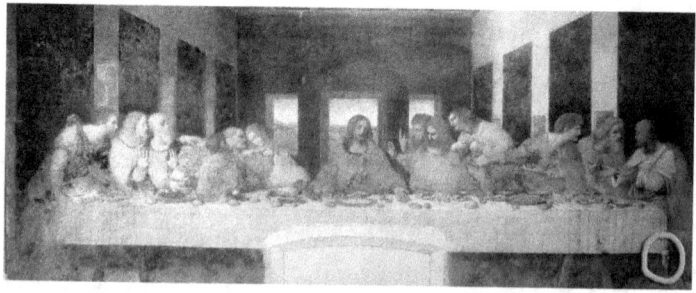

Between the part on which the supper is set out and the

part that hangs in the foreground, the large tablecloth covers a surface that is almost equal to the space dedicated to all the human figures.

From that time onwards, it took all my attention.

I had already read some interpretations of a detail that was clearly symbolic; the knot on the right of the tablecloth, a detail that is no longer visible on the left side of the painting, deteriorated by time, but which originally was probably present on both sides. The knot evokes complex meanings in almost all cultures; from the mystical 'infinite knot' of the Celts and the Buddhists to the custom, very common in modern usage, that helps us to remember something, the classic knot in the handkerchief. At that moment, though, looking at the tablecloth, I found myself thinking of the role of knots in the clothing of orthodox Jews: the *Tzitzit*.

The significance of these knots in the Old Testament is unequivocal. The rule regarding them can be found in the following excerpt from Numbers (15, 38-40):

"And the Lord spake unto Moses, saying, "Speak unto the children of Israel, and bid them that they make them fringes in the borders of their garments throughout their generations, and that they put upon the fringe of the borders a ribband of blue: And it shall be unto you for a fringe, that ye may look upon it, and remember all the commandments of the Lord, and do them; and that ye seek not after your own heart and your own eyes, after which ye use to go a whoring: That ye may remember, and do all my commandments, and be holy unto your God."

In Hebrew, the *Tzitzit* are the tassels or fringes that,

according to the command given by God to Moses, were to be worn attached to the four corners of the *Tallit*, the Jewish prayer shawl. These long tassels, which include a sequence of knots, are made in silk, or linen or wool if the *Tallit* is in linen or wool. There are four threads, doubled and knotted, of which one is blue or violet, recalling the four letters of the *Holy Name* of God, the sacred Tetragrammaton.

So what did Leonardo mean to 'recall' with those knots at the corners of the tablecloth, as if it were a single, enormous *Tallit*?

While I was thinking about this, I reflected on the fact that *The Last Supper* represented the crucial point of Passover. Jesus and the Apostles had come together in that first floor room for the *Pesach Seder*, the ritual supper that commemorates the night when the Israelites were freed from slavery in Egypt, the night of the Exodus.

Here I need to explain that during this research in my every thought I always bore in mind the image of Leonardo as the son of a Jewish woman, in other words, as a child growing up – certainly when he saw Caterina, but perhaps not only then – in an atmosphere steeped in ancient Hebrew wisdom.

Why do I say, 'but perhaps not only then?'

For two reasons; The first is because the Jewish community in fifteenth century Tuscany – before the arrival of the exiles expelled from Spain in 1492 – was small and close-knit, as religious minorities always are, especially when persecuted. The Jews, including Caterina's parents, all knew each other especially because they were not, indeed, related to each other and in addition, were not permitted to marry *gentiles*. It is a reasonable supposition, therefore, that through his Mother's family, Leonardo knew Jewish people not only in Vinci, but also in Florence.

The second reason is that precisely in the Florence of the Medici, from the 1460s onwards, a real intellectual passion for the Hebrew language and culture had became widespread, as it had for the Kabbalah, the esoteric Jewish tradition. This 'fashion' was the due, on one hand, to the open-mindedness of Cosimo, Piero and Lorenzo de' Medici, who, as I have mentioned earlier, made of Florence – a cultural crossroads where intellectuals and artists met from all over the world. Additionally, from the arrival in the city of dozens of important Rabbis with their families, first from Constantinople – which had fallen into the hands of the Muslims in 1453 – and secondly from Spain under the devoutly Catholic Isabella and Ferdinando, who expelled both Moors and Jews in 1492 (three years before Leonardo started to paint *The Last Supper*).

Much research has been dedicated to this Florentine 'golden age', which reached its peak under the enlightened governance of Lorenzo the Magnificent.

These were the years in which illustrious humanists were working in Florence, including Marsilio Ficino (to whom Cosimo entrusted the translation from the Greek of the *Corpus Hermeticum*, a work attributed to the mythical Hermes Trismegistus), and Count Pico della Mirandola, the 'child prodigy' of the Florentine aristocracy with a legendary memory, who died before his time in 1492.

While Leonardo was at Verrocchio's studio, minds of this caliber often called on the Rabbis in Florence to teach them the language of the Old Testament, but above all, to reveal to them the secrets of the Kabbalah. For the moment, I would just like to emphasize the importance of the symbols used by the artist in this and also others of his works.

I was convinced that something of that culture, recollections of words and ideas learned in childhood, must seep out of the painting.

It must also be remembered that Leonardo's time was that in which the Inquisition was at the height of its power, with the continual hunting down of any forms of heresy, a time when sympathies for a religious culture other than Christianity could take people *straight to the stake*.

But if, in Leonardo's Florence, a rich nobleman like Pico could happily take no notice of the Dominicans of the Inquisition, the same could not be said of a young artist 'with no surname'.

Leonardo never revealed to anyone that he was an illegitimate son, nor did he ever speak to anyone about his personal religious convictions. He had full knowledge of the Christian Bible and the New Testament, no artist of the period could have been ignorant of them, but without a doubt his opinions regarding God – His name, His image – were different from those 'in force' and common at that time and were closer to those that his Jewish lineage had passed on to him.

The Dominican friars would have examined every tiny detail of the fresco in *their* refectory, so Leonardo needed to be very careful when planning *The Last Supper*, to conceal any 'unorthodox' content from the suspicious eyes of 'God's bloodhounds'.

Could this be the reason why he took so long to paint his first adult Christ, while the Baby Jesus was by now a recurring theme in his artistic 'repertoire'?

So many questions. In any case, for the moment, I could not find any trace of suspected musical notation.

I was asking, but, the fresco remained silent.

II

I continued to look carefully at the tablecloth and at each minute detail of what was placed upon it; plates, glasses, fruit, bread. Suddenly a particular detail stood out, in reality an unusual combination, apparently a coincidence – the majority of the bread rolls were placed in such a way as to match the vertical lines of the tablecloth.

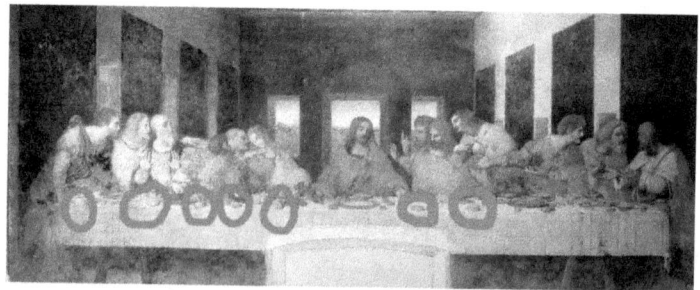

I noted too that the majority of the bread rolls were of similar size, only a few were smaller. And not only this, the rolls were almost all arranged at the same distance from each other. At a first glance, this may just seem to be an accident, but, I thought the artist could not 'improvise' the size and position of the loaves as he painted along, he would have had to decide before starting the work, thereby placing them in his preparatory drawings and even in the earlier sketches.

Now, anyone who has ever had a lesson in musical notation knows that a vertical line, usually called a stem, represents a note. The duration of a note is not only provided by the size of the head, but also from the shape of the vertical line. The folds in the tablecloth with those bread rolls at the top started to look to me like musical notes.

But no, I said to myself, it was just me wanting to see music there at all costs!

Then I noticed that Leonardo had painted some fish in the plates.

This, of course, as for others before me, made me think of the episode of the loaves and fishes as recounted in the Gospels. I had been convinced, right from the start of my research, that my observation of the painting would need to be combined with an in-depth reading of the passages from the *Holy Scripture* that were the basis of every detail of the scene.

This was not only in order to enter into the religious – I might say almost devotional – spirit with which Leonardo confronted such a dramatic subject, but also because I knew that he had certainly discussed every detail of *The Last Supper* with the Dominican friars who were the 'masters of the house' of Santa Maria delle Grazie.

Some of the researchers who espouse the thesis that Leonardo was a secret 'heretic', maintain that the friars 'supervised' him, precisely to prevent him introducing into the work any details or symbols that were not orthodox and that did not conform to the doctrine and interpretation – or to use the theological term, the exegesis – of that episode from the *Gospels*.

We should remember that Leonardo took almost four years to complete the fresco: if he were unsure about how to represent some detail or other from the holy text, he had all the time he could possibly need to study the matter in depth. Also, he was surrounded by monks, whom we would refer to today as 'experts' in this field.

In support of this assumption, I quote Fra' Girolamo Gattico (1574-1646), taken from his 'Catalogue of all those who with approved and legitimate superiority have ruled the monastery of Santa Maria delle Grazie of Milan':

"1495. The father Fra' Vincenzo Bandello da Castel Novo di Scrivia was the sixteenth prior. He was an extremely important person among the principals of the Dominican Order, excellent in letters and a master of Theology. When he became the new prior of the monastery, he found a certain atmosphere of disorder as regards the Dominican rule. He knew how to restore order and how to manage the monastery very well, so that he became the trusted person of Count Ludovico, who kept the appointment for him for a long time."

I then started to re-read the passages from the New Testament that related to the feeding of the five thousand, comparing the four evangelists' different versions:

The Gospel according to St. Matthew: The feeding of the five thousand (14:13), Last Supper (26:17);

The Gospel according to St. Mark: The feeding of the five thousand (6:34), Last Supper (14:12);

The Gospel according to St. Luke: The feeding of the five thousand (9:12), Last Supper (22:7);

The Gospel according to St. John: The feeding of the five thousand (6:1), The traitor revealed (13:1).

I realized that the description of *The Last Supper* which was closest to the scene represented by Leonardo was the one provided by the Gospel according to St. John. Without a doubt this account was his source, if only because of the way Leonardo had chosen to identify *'he who would betray Jesus'*.

In fact in the supper at Bethany (John, 12:4-6), we read:

"Then saith one of his disciples, Judas Iscariot, Simon's son, which should betray him, why was not this ointment sold for three hundred pence, and given to the poor? This he said, not that he cared for the poor; but because he was a thief, and had the bag, and bare what was put therein."

And again in 'The Traitor revealed' (John, 13: 27-29):

"And after the sop Satan entered into him. Then said Jesus unto him, That thou doest, do quickly. Now no man at the table knew for what intent he spake this unto him. For some of them thought, because Judas had the bag, that Jesus had said unto him, buy those things that we have need of against

the feast; or, that he should give something to the poor."

In both passages, what distinguished the figure of Judas was the purse or bag, a detail not mentioned in the other Gospels. In *The Last Supper*, the fifth Apostle from the left is holding a bag in his hand; the traitor can only be him. It is well known that the precise moment represented by Leonardo occurs immediately after the phrase spoken by Jesus, *"Verily, verily, I say unto you, that one of you shall betray me"*. What Leonardo decided to portray was the Apostles' reaction to those words.

Two verses after that phrase, John writes:

"Now there was leaning on Jesus' bosom one of his disciples, whom Jesus loved. Simon Peter therefore beckoned to him, that he should ask who it should be of whom he spake." (John 13:23-24).

This gesture of Peter's, too, whispering in the ear of the favored Apostle sitting at Jesus' right hand, is clear in the painting and confirms that the main source, if not the only source, used by Leonardo was the St. John's Gospel. This conclusion and the certainty it gave me in using that Gospel in order to resolve any doubts I might have had on other contents of the fresco, was very important for my research.

Taken with the idea that the vertical lines could represent notes, which could be an allusion to the musical notation I sought, I decided to use a copy of the painting to superimpose black notes on to the bread rolls, so that a line of melody could be identified that I could play on my piano.

In order to understand simply and intuitively what a melody consists of, imagine you are whistling or singing your favorite song. The sung part is the melody of the song, while the chords supporting it are its harmonic structure.

No melody can exist if it is not linked to a harmonic structure. Even the music encoded by Leonardo in the painting – if this is really the case – would have needed, like all music, to have both a melodic and a harmonic structure.

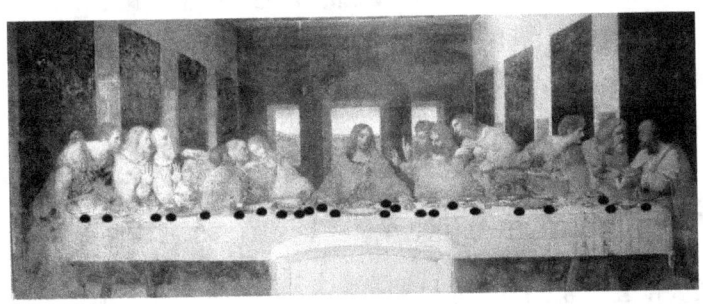

I looked at the sequence of little black balls that I had placed in the position of the bread rolls on the table. At first, I could not see where the first note was. If I had wanted to write in a melodic key, with respect to the treble clef, this would have been a **mi [E]**, starting low, from the first line of the stave.

Here I would like to draw your attention to a basic element, in a way, it is the keystone of my whole research.

The **mi [E]** is the third of the seven notes of the musical scale and the number three was represented so many times in my analyses, taking on a role and significance that were ever more precise, that in the end I identified it as the 'matrix', of the enigma, created by Leonardo.

Obviously, the number three symbolizes the *Holy Trinity* and Leonardo had taken it as a 'master key' for each stage of his work, both in the part that can be seen and the part that cannot. I did several tests on the piano, following the line of the bread rolls in the painting and read as notes starting from a mi [**E**], but with no success. No matter how hard I tried to transform the notation I had transcribed with the bread rolls, alone, I could not extract anything that could be called a line of melody.

I remembered the fact that Leonardo used to write from right to left, but even when transcribed again and played the Notes in reverse, nothing came out that made any musical sense.

I was disappointed and angry with myself.

The route of the bread rolls had seemed to be the right one, but it had turned into a 'blind alley'.

I started to give in to pessimism!

Even if a line of melody had come out of it, I said to myself, where was the information that could have allowed me to decide on its tempo?

It was naïve of me to think that a genius of Leonardo's pedigree would have been satisfied with a puzzle of such banality; "*each bread roll is a note, now go and play it*".

Come on, there must have been something quite different to hide the secret; puzzles, anagrams, numerical sequences, Kabbalist Acrostics (Coded Text in the form of Poems or lines where certain letters – usually the first in each line form a name or word).

I had been ambitious and presumptuous – would I never succeed!?

III

Leonardo was thirty years old when he arrived in Milan with his travelling companion, friend and pupil, Atalante Migliorotti. With over one hundred thousand inhabitants, the capital of the Sforza family's dominion was one of the largest cities in Europe and a very strong pole of attraction for artists. In his excellent biography of Leonardo, Bruno Nardini tells us that Lorenzo de' Medici decided to send Leonardo to Milan after receiving two separate requests from Ludovico 'the Moor' Sforza.

Nardini narrates how this mission was entrusted to the young artist:

"Leonardo, at this point you can only prepare for your departure" Lorenzo said to him. "The Duke of Milan is looking for a lyre player and I know that you have an extraordinary silver one, which you will give to me and I will present to him as a gift. In this way, by sending you to Milan, I will do him a double service: I will show him your

talent as a musician and you will make him a statue of his father on horseback."

These were Lorenzo's clever and inimitable moves.

They formed part of his political strategy and no-one knew better than him how to choose the most suitable tools. Together with works of art, he also exported artists, happily sending them to the courts of Italy and Europe as special envoys of a culture and an epoch that in Florence were called Humanism and that would later, across the world, be called the Renaissance.

The year before Leonardo arrived in Milan, Ludovico the Moor had taken power by eliminating the guardians of his young nephew, Gian Galeazzo Maria, who had become Duke at the age of seven in 1476, after his father's assassination. Gian Galeazzo would continue to be the legitimate Duke until 1494, but was kept 'under house arrest' by his uncle in Pavia, where he died at only twenty-five years of age; many actually thought Ludovico had had him poisoned. This is one example of the 'dark side' of the Italian Renaissance, the ruthlessness of the political plots, which often even exceeded that of the more distant past.

Two years earlier, in Rome, rumors had spread that the new Borgia Pope, Alexander VI, a Spaniard, had even had his predecessor, Innocent VIII, poisoned.

In terms of its chronology, Nardini's reconstruction matches that of *l'Anonimo Gaddiano*, who writes:

"He was about thirty years of age when he was sent to the Duke in Milan by Lorenzo the Magnificent, in the company of Atalante Migliorotti, and he took with him a lyre of his own

invention, since he was an excellent performer on this instrument".

But *l'Anonimo* and Nardini contradict one of the main sources on Leonardo's life (apart from his own writings); Giorgio Vasari, who had become famous as the 'first art historian'. According to Vasari, twelve years after his arrival, Leonardo still had the instrument, and it was still a 'strange and new thing'.

In fact, Vasari writes:

"On the death of Giovanni Galeazzo, in 1494, Ludovico the Moor succeeded him as Duke and the same called Leonardo to play the lyre, an instrument much loved by the Duke. Leonardo brought his strange instrument in the form of a horse skull, made for the most part in silver in order to enrich the sound, a strange and new thing. He not only played better than anyone else, but was also judged to be the best improviser of rhymes".

In any case, whether it was in 1482 or 1494 that Leonardo first appeared before the Milanese Court with that lyre, from Vasari's account, we understand that he played his strange instrument in various competitions, beating the other musicians by a long chalk and winning the heart of the Duke who was also a great lover of music and a virtuoso at playing the *lira da braccio*, an instrument similar in shape to a violin.

The idea emerges that Leonardo created his own strange instrument with the precise aim of causing a stir at court, and of being accepted there. He delivered the instrument to the Duke in person, obtaining the amazed reaction he desired, and won the music competition, thus ensuring that he also gained the Duke's attention.

The lyre of the Renaissance period was a stringed instrument played on the arm, used to play lines of melody or provide chords to accompany the voice.

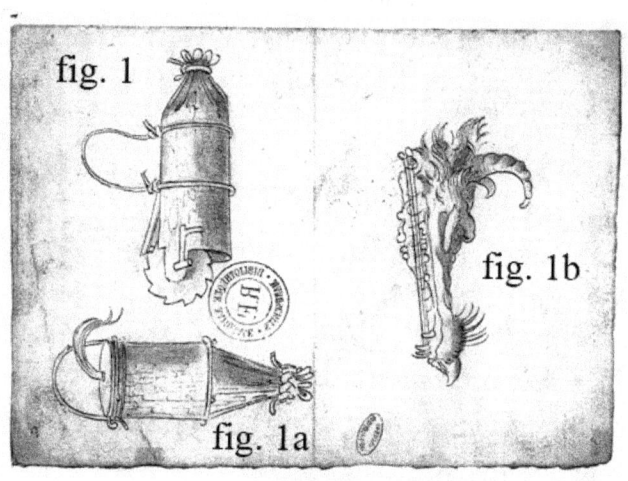

Ashburnham Codex I - drawing MS 2037 B. N. Cr. (cranium)

Another instrument for accompanying songs was the lute, but the lyre was considered the ideal accompaniment during the prologues of plays, such as *La favola di Orfeo* by Poliziano (1480), and *Comedia di Amicizia* by Iacopo Nardi (1512), whose final stage direction is "*The stanzas are sung with the lyre before the Signoria when the aforesaid play was performed*".

Odd-shaped instruments were very much in fashion at the time, but despite numerous hypotheses and assumptions, no notes or sketches of this strange instrument have ever been found.

The only exception is a drawing of a composite skull,

somewhat similar to the head of a wolf or a horse, but which could also be that of a devil or a dragon. In the lower part of the skull, which acts as the flat, three or four strings are shown, stretched between the tuning pegs hammered into the lower part of the head, with something similar on the perpendicular separations indicating the position of the fingers, as is normally seen on guitars. In all probability, this was a rough sketch intended for those making the instruments for court entertainment.

In addition to the profound sense of harmony and rhythm in his drawings, which in itself is evidence of the role of music in his mental processes, Leonardo's interest in music is often expressed in his manuscripts, almost always in the form of examples of his 'frenzy' of inventing.

He designed and built musical instruments to make certain performance techniques easier or even 'automatic'.

His research on acoustics led him to improve some instruments and invent others, such as the 'Glissando Flute', the bell with a keyboard and the 'Organ Viola', a stringed instrument with a keyboard activated by a wheel, which, moving forwards and backwards, made the strings vibrate.

Leonardo wanted to overcome the limited expressive capacity of the keyboard instruments of the period, he wanted to invent an instrument which would enable complex symphonies to be performed in such a way as not to sacrifice the nuances and varied modulations of each individual note.

Another example of a truly futuristic instrument is a drawing made between 1490 and 1491 of an automatic drum fixed to a cart, which could be activated by the movement of the cart's wheels, simply by pulling it or by means of a lateral crank, the complicated mechanism caused two vertical cylinders with pegs attached to rotate which, in turn, caused the ten hammers (five on each side) to move and strike the large drum.

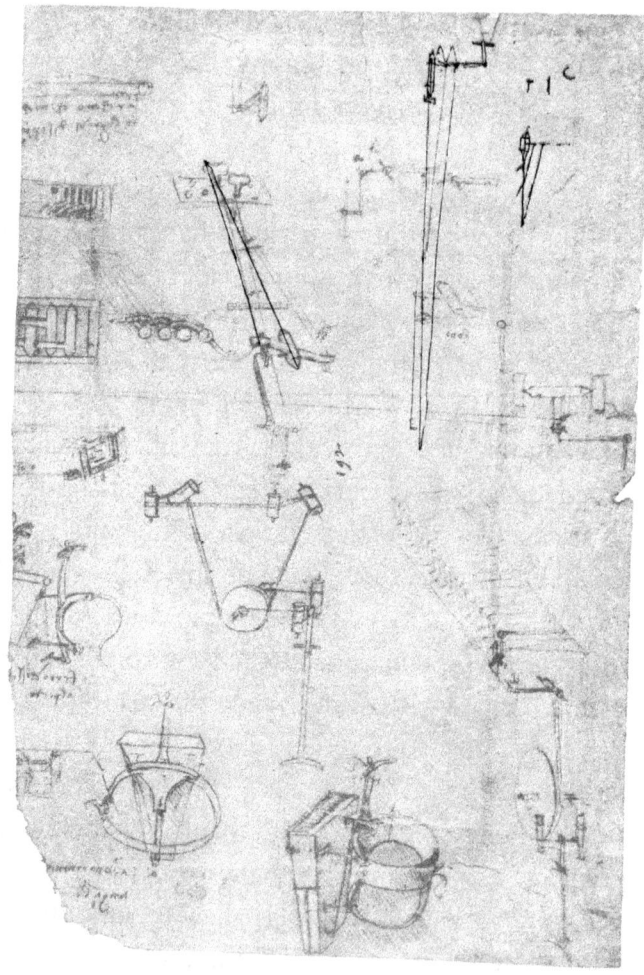

Atlantic Codex, sheet 93 Recto - design of mechanical viola

By changing the position of the pegs in the cylinders the rhythm of the music was also changed, demonstrating

Leonardo's profound knowledge of the relationships between time, movement and musical rhythm.

In addition, the historian Enrico Magni Dufflocq also writes:

"A roller with spikes was one of Leonardo's favorite themes. He also applied it to organ pipes, the hammers of a carillon, he even used it to perform a canon with variable intervals. At least twice, in the Arundel Codex and the Windsor Collection, he formulated a canon mechanically, adding some musical notes to it, the only ones written in his own hand which remain (nos. 12.697 and 12.699 of the Windsor Collection). However, by proposing a canon, Leonardo offers proof that he was an all-round musician".

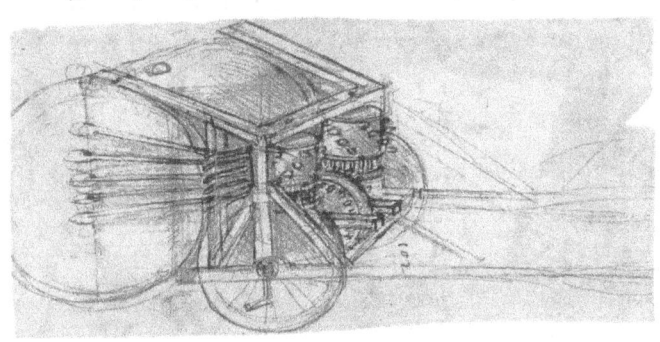

Atlantic Codex, sheet 837 Recto C – automatic drum

A few years later, Leonardo had already become friendly with Lorenzo Gusnasco di Pavia, who built and traded in Organs, Hand Organs, Harpsichords, Lutes, Violas, *Lire da Braccio* and various other instruments. He worked together with the merchant so that he could take advantage of di Pavia's advice, both for his own experiments on the propagation of sound and in order to complete the various drums and flutes he was continually thinking up.

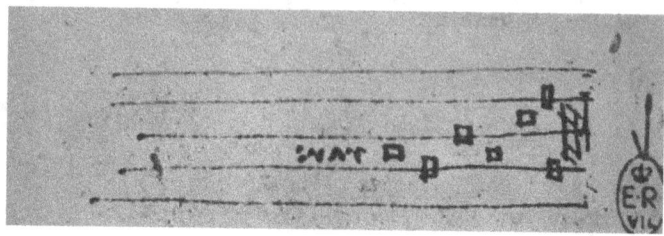

Musical phrase from the Windsor Collection – Sheets 12.697 and 12.699

In the large number of puzzles that he enjoyed inventing and which fill many pages of his manuscripts, he often makes use of musical notes. On one line of music, for example, after the clef, he drew a hook (the Italian word for which is *amo*), then inserted a series of notes – re sol [in English called so] la mi fa re mi – followed by the Italian word *rare* [rare]; he then marked a hyphen, then – la sol mi fa sol – and the word *lecita* [lawful]. The whole line should read: *"Amo-re sol la mi fa re-mirare, la sol mi fa sol-lecita"* [Love alone makes me look again, alone stimulates me]. In another puzzle of the same period, he wrote unconventionally, using the same system, *"L'amore mi fa sollazzare"* [Love gives me enjoyment].

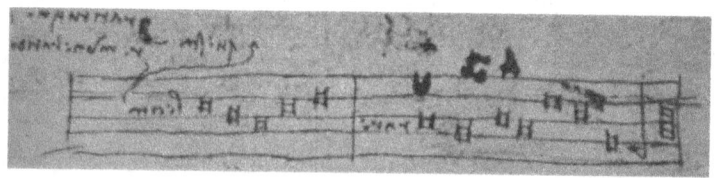

(Windsor Collection – Sheet 12.697 and 12.699 – Leonardo's puzzle: AMO-RE-SOL-LA – etc...)

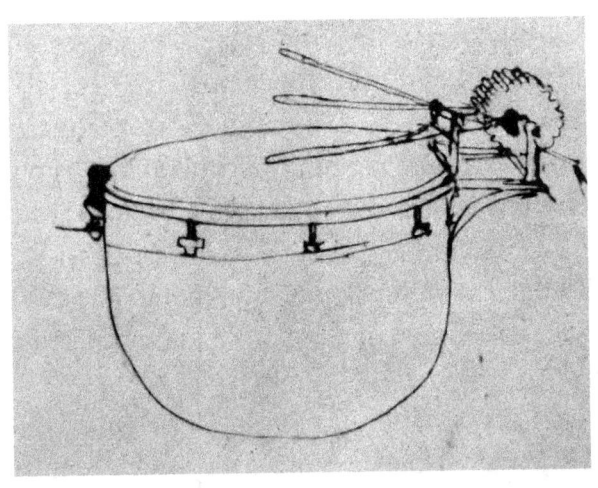

Mechanical drum - Atlantic Codex, sheet 335 Recto-C

Another trace of Leonardo the musician is the idea that the Florentine genius attended and was quite well accepted in Milanese musical circles, which in those years included illustrious maestri such as the French composer Josquin des Près. For a long time it was thought that the portrait painted by Leonardo in his first stay in Milan, now kept at the *Pinacoteca Ambrosiana di Milano*, was of Duke Ludovico, but there is now a different hypothesis.

The musician in the portrait is holding a folded piece of paper in his hand, on which the semi-erased words "*CANT... ANG...*", can be read, followed by a musical score. Leonardo's quotation could refer to the *Canticum Angelicum*, the title of a work by the celebrated composer from nearby Lodi, Franchino Gaffurio, a sublime humanist and contemporary of Leonardo.

Gaffurio codified the polyphonic liturgical performances of the Cathedral Choir to make them more suitable for the religious services, he reorganized the *Schola Cantorum* of

Milan Cathedral and composed many Masses, Motets and Hymns. In 1492, Ludovico called upon him to teach music at the *Gymnasium* school he had created. According to the most recent opinions, this painting is therefore a portrait of Gaffurio, with whom Leonardo had a deep and sincere friendship. Gaffurio also wrote a series of musical treatises which became widely popular. Among these were the *Theorica musicae* (published in 1480 and re-edited in 1492), the *Practica musicae* (1496) and the *De harmonia musicorum instrumentorum opus* (1500), which investigate the phenomenon of music from every angle, but above all promote a theoretical concept of harmony.

Indeed, it appears that these treatises on the theory of music were illustrated by Leonardo.

Leonardo's first ten years in Milan were those in which, at the Sforza Court, playing the lute and making *frottole*, the poetic texts intended for singing and especially loved by Ludovico's very young wife, Beatrice d'Este, were in full bloom.

It is said that Leonardo had a spellbinding singing voice when he improvised. He was certainly a protagonist in the musical life of the *Castello Sforzesco*, a good performer and a good teacher.

However, Leonardo had no intention of making a career for himself in the field of music: he continued to play exclusively for the pleasure of those close to him, his most intimate friends and on rare occasions, at festivities at Ludovico's Court.

He was able to write music, but never transcribed his own improvisations.

Leonardo's musical ideas can be found spread over

numerous pages of his notebooks in an almost casual fashion. His musical writing was accompanied by pictures and the few musical notations he made, discovered above all within various puzzles, are found together with drawings and notes for projects of various kinds, such as those in the pages of the Windsor Collection.

Beneath the stave, Leonardo solves these puzzles, made up in part of the names of the notes on the line, often with additions and corrections, confirming that his instinct for experimentation, research and invention extended also to music.

By investigating Leonardo's relationship with music I had most importantly found confirmation of a quality in the man that would become proverbial: his capacity to absorb within the briefest time any form of thought that he encountered, be it artistic or scientific.

In this, Leonardo was – and is still considered today – the archetypal Renaissance Man.

IV

I quickly recovered from this first disappointment – there would be others on the long journey of my investigation. If, on the one hand, I had perhaps underestimated the scale of Leonardo's enigma, on the other, I had nevertheless made the first step. The idea of transcribing and performing the musical phrase extracted from the bread rolls in the treble clef had allowed me to establish that the first note must be a **mi [E]**, i.e. the third note of the octave.

This had confirmed some of my ideas on the role of the number three, both in the visible painting and in the hidden enigma.

If the number three was the *Keystone* to decoding Leonardo's music, I thought, it must resonate widely in each element of the painting, not only in one single point.

And then, thinking it over again, studying the arrangement of the bread rolls on the *Holy Table* had led me to understand the symbolic and theological dimension that they represented. All in all, the bread rolls were the correct point of departure, I had only gone wrong in thinking that *they were the whole story*.

I needed to look for other elements, other parts of the hidden score, and I needed to do so always bearing in mind the number three.

With this attitude, I had started to look at the arrangement of the Apostles; there were six on the right and six on the left of the central, isolated figure of Christ, and they were further subdivided into four groups of three.

Here I must digress for a moment to mention the unusual choice Leonardo made to represent a single instant of a scene in chaotic movement – to stop time, one would say, as in the frame of a film. In the past many critics have credited Caravaggio, who was painting a whole century after Leonardo, with the conceptual convention of the cinema, the idea of showing figures in a frame as if time had stopped while they were moving, an effect now known today as a 'freeze-frame'. Well, just looking at *the Last Supper* is enough to understand where Caravaggio – another of the greats in the history of art – took his inspiration for painting 'freeze-frames'.

The innovation is doubly important in the case of this particular painting, because in all the *Last Suppers* created until then (of which there were many, starting from the first centuries AD), each Apostle was stationary in his own space (with Judas' space always outside the group).

Leonardo, however, created the image of movement, indeed, projecting a human tumult. Every figure in the scene, with the exception of Jesus, is moving. Some are standing, some are getting to their feet in amazement, some are apparently asking for explanations, by the gestures of their hands.

Leonardo 'wrote' the *Last Supper* as if it were a theatrical play and arranged the gestures of the apostles in order to transform them into the desired divisions of the space, controlled by the sources of light from the front, sides and back. At the time when the fresco was completed, no sacred representation had ever broken with tradition in this way.

Another important difference in Leonardo's method was that all painters at that time would make sketches, drafts or complete drawings of the work that they had been commissioned to produce.

Once the sketch was accepted by the Patron, the artist went ahead with the work. Leonardo, however, never showed anything of the kind to the Duke or the Prior.

His idea of the painting was in his own head and there it would stay until others could see it too.

Instead of following the custom of copying from paper, which would have obliged him to draw his painting first, Leonardo had worked out another way of 'transferring' the image to the wall, by using shadows created through a sort of projector. Since 1481, when he was not even thirty years old, he had already started research on light. Drawing on one of his many pages of notes a man who displayed an armillary sphere by means of a 'Perspectograph'.

Many years later, in 1490, he furthered his study of the phenomena produced by light so that he could make use of it in the paintings he was undertaking. *De ombra e lume* [On shadows and light] was the title he gave his notes on this fascinating and mysterious subject.

He noted and drew studies on the body of a shadow, on luminous rays, on the dependence of the shape of a shadow on that of the objects (and on its exceptions), on perfect and imperfect shadows.

He even created a sort of camera obscura, in order to test the 'optical principles' he inferred from his experiments (not so different from those that, two centuries later, Isaac Newton codified in his 'Opticks'). He used devices that he built himself, to show that the light forming the images had a punctiform source, that it spread in a straight line and that its rays varied in quality and clarity after coming out of an opening, etc.

Here is one of his notes:

"When the intermediary wall between the source of light and the screen is close to the source of light and to the screen itself, the projection on to the screen takes the form of the opening".

At times I wonder where such great minds found the courage – some would say the audacity – to consider the phenomena of nature alone, trusting in their own ability to understand them.

I can imagine Leonardo (or Aristotle, or Galileo, or Newton) taking a piece of card with a hole cut out of it, placing it between a candle and a wall, starting to move it forward and back – closer to the flame, then further away – observing what happened on the wall and simply... thinking!

The fact of believing that by observing a phenomenon and *reasoning*, it is possible to understand what is happening and why, is, in my opinion, the main characteristic of human genius.

Perhaps the idea of projecting on to the wall of the refectory came to him by observing his own shadow projected on to the floor by the light that filtered from a window. Such a common event, to which no-one gave much importance. In this too, genius can be distinguished from more ordinary minds.

A genius reaches a new idea from one that already exists, while more ordinary minds are satisfied with what they already know, without asking too many whys and wherefores.

Leonardo wrote:

"Who of you has never thrown a pebble into a lake and then watched the circles born of it? But how many of you wondered why the waves do not break when they meet, but intersect each other?"

And in another short note:

"The first picture was only a line, which surrounded the shadow of the man thrown by the sun on to the walls'. Or, again: 'the shape of the shadow has become a shining body."

Leonardo's idea, therefore, was to use the light projected from a source placed behind cut out shapes, in order to bring the shapes of the Apostles onto the wall in proportions that were larger than they would be naturally, but perfect, much more precise than attempting to enlarge them by copying from a drawing. This method also lent itself well to the task because he intended to represent most of the Apostles in profile, while Christ would be seen from the front. The working of the projector he had devised was very simple. The light was placed at the back of a wooden box with a central hole, thus permitting a play of shadows to be created according to the objects that were placed in front of it. First of all, Leonardo did some simple experiments with his hands, making animal shapes appear on the wall.

He soon realized that there was a problem: the more distant the outlines were from the wall, the less focused they became.

He needed to cage the light and concentrate it.

Simply by lining the inside of the box / projector with mirrors, it was possible to concentrate the light and strengthen it a hundred times, so that it emerged without deviation and with the greater power gathered from the reflection.

Another reason why I was certain he had used this system, was that this was the only way to conceal his secret, which must not stay on any piece of paper, even as a rough sketch.

I like to think, but it is just my own hypothesis, that for the outline of Christ he may have used his own shadow (and afterwards, perhaps, even his own features), because in that figure of a man in exile, an unacknowledged prophet, in that inner solitude, Leonardo could recognize himself.

However, let us return to my original comments on the arrangement of the Apostles.

My readers will by now have understood that the reason why Leonardo grouped them in sets of three was because that number is the 'Cornerstone' of the whole painting.

As I mentioned in the first chapter, the number three refers first of all to the *Holy Trinity*, in other words, the mystery of the nature of the Triune God.

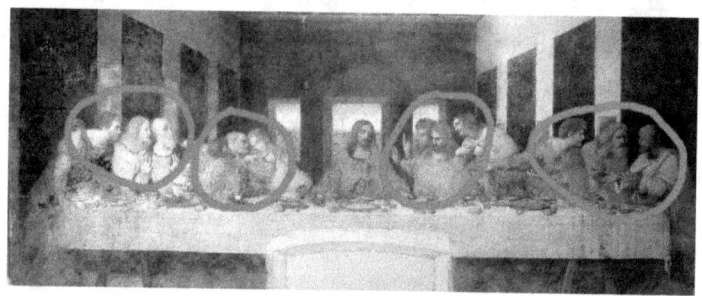

But just to take a few examples from the Bible, *three* are the hours of Jesus' agony, from the sixth to the ninth hour. He ceased to live, therefore, at 3 p.m. He was *thirty-three* when he sacrificed himself in order to redeem mankind from sin, and the resurrection took place *three* days after his death. Judas betrayed him for *thirty* pieces of silver, and it was *three* times that Peter denied Jesus between the time of his arrest and the cockcrow (John, 13:36).

I could cite other examples, but I think these are enough to show the symbolic importance of the number three in the Gospels.

I had no doubt that Leonardo divided the Apostles into groups of three in order to make a reference both to Christian dogma and also to the key to the puzzle. My mind went round in circles thinking about the relationship that Leonardo had created between the figures in The Last Supper.

Four groups of three, four divided by three, three divided by four.

I hit me all of a sudden - three divided by four!

Three divided by four means three quarters! "3/4!"

And what if in that arrangement, Leonardo had hidden the

time signature for playing the music?

This inspiration led me away from the direction of melodic structure and instead, towards the rhythm of the music, whose existence I was guessing at.

Giving my attention to the overall painting changed the nature of what I was seeing. All at once, in my eyes the arrangement of the Apostles became the main rhythm of the inner movement of the music.

The movement of the twelve figures already determined the rhythmic progress of the pictorial representation, where better to hide also the time signature for playing the musical representation, too?

What is a time signature in music, after all, except the metrical division of a score?

Later, I would also find symbolic relationships linked to a time signature of **3/4**: for example, it could be a reference to the day and month of Christ's death (3 April); or, adding the two figures together, we have seven, the symbol of the completeness and perfection of the Divinity in both the Jewish and Christian traditions. Moreover, a part from any symbolism, **3/4** is a time signature that is fully compatible with the majority of the music of the fourteenth and fifteenth centuries.

In fact, contrary to secular music, which was binary, the time signature for playing sacred music was tertiary. At that point, a question came to my mind quite spontaneously, the same question that any musician would ask if someone said to him: 'the time signature of the piece is "**3/4**". That is; how many bars (or measures) did there need to be?

When I had thought of the theological link between the bread rolls represented on the table and the Eucharist, the miracle of the multiplication of loaves and fish came to my mind, as recounted in St. John's *Gospel*.

Almost instinctively, as 'multiplication' and '3/4' went round in my mind, I did the most natural thing in the world and multiplied **3** by **4**. In the end, did the four groups of three not result in a total of twelve Apostles?

It may seem banal, or even a coincidence, but it is not.

The greatest philosophers and mathematicians have shown the arithmetical symmetries that mean there are twelve months of the year, twelve signs of the Zodiac, twelve tribes of Israel and twelve Holy Apostles.

To me the matter seemed yet more obvious and elegant, in my opinion, those twelve men were the *Custodians of the Music*.

At last I had reached a concrete result, even if it was still hypothetical and provisional. The music was in the time signature of **3/4** and was divided into twelve bars. The indisputable fact remained that, in Leonardo's time, division into bars did not yet exist, but the melody nevertheless had to have a precise duration, which I would have no difficulty in translating into the current system of writing in bars.

I immediately thought that Leonardo might have allocated a precise role to each Apostle, attributing to each one a symbolic function in visually representing the time signature of the musical phrase.

Influenced once again by the central role of the number three in every aspect of my research, my attention, almost without thinking, was drawn to the third Apostle from the left, Andrew. I noticed that the palms of his hands were turned outwards, towards the person looking at the painting.

In reality, this gesture of the Apostle simply meant, "Ah,

this has nothing to do with me!".

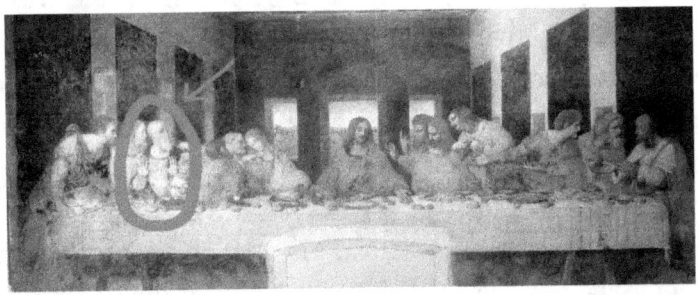

It was the gesture of someone blameless, someone who has nothing to hide and does not feel implicated by Jesus' words:

"When Jesus had thus said, he was troubled in spirit, and testified, and said: "Verily, verily, I say unto you, that one of you shall betray me." (John, 13:21).

I was struck by the fact that beneath Andrew's hands there were two of the vertical lines that had started me off on my research – and, almost in line with these, there were also two bread rolls of similar size. Suddenly, I had second thoughts about the meaning of the musical notation I had attributed to the bread rolls. Andrew's gesture, too, now seemed to have meaning, linked to the music.

I had the impression that the Apostle was offering me a precise clue, as if in that precise point, something – perhaps the music itself – needed to slow down or continue more broadly. After all, this is the other meaning of the gesture with the palms of raised hands turned outward; put the brakes on, don't hurry, slow down. If, in fact, the bread rolls represented the progress of the music and this needed to be played from right to left in accordance with Leonardo's way of writing, it would certainly have been just in line with the Apostle Andrew that the music would have been approaching its end. It would be at this point that the music would need to go more slowly, as in the musical indication *adagio*, when the music was about to finish.

But there was more.

I knew that each Apostle had his own personality, his own character and a precise role in the context of the narrative and I was fascinated by the idea that they also had a role to play in the context of the music. In short, Leonardo had made each Apostle react in a way that was consistent with his personality as it is described in the Gospels. But in the 'invisible' part, in the puzzle, he had given each one a role that was in fact related to the movement of the hidden music

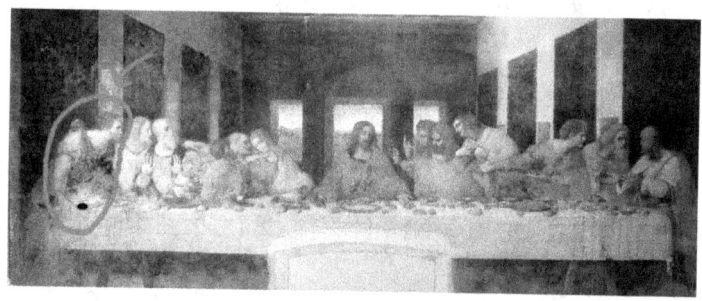

I noted, for example, that just next to the hand of the first Apostle on the left, Bartholomew, Leonardo had placed a bread roll that was of very similar size to the two bread rolls placed beneath Andrew's hands.

Bartholomew almost seems to be picking up the bread, a gesture that could also have a meaning compatible with the presumed movement of the music; it was as if something needed to be interrupted at that point. Besides, if Leonardo had written the music from right to left, the most plausible hypothesis was that the phrase needed to be drawn to its end close to Bartholomew's hand.

Unconsciously, I had identified a relationship between the bread rolls arranged on the tablecloth and the hands of the Apostles. Perhaps this was the element missing from my first reading.

Perhaps it was the bread rolls and the hands *together* that brought life to the music.

V

Leonardo had been living in Milan for over thirteen years when he started painting *The Last Supper*. These were rich and productive years, in which his fame grew and his interests broadened. He continued to gather together the numerous sheets on which he made his notes, Treatises, Drawings, Plans and inventions that would become the 'Codices' we know today.

He painted his friend, the musician Gaffurio in 1485, his third year in Milan and the same year in which the second part of the *Forster Codex* was started, while the *Paris Manuscript B* was started in 1488. As we saw earlier, his musical notes appeared only in the puzzles, which became increasingly numerous and difficult over time.

Professor Pedretti maintains that there are as many as 150 in a single sheet in the *Windsor Codex,* which he dates between 1487 and 1490. In Milan, Leonardo took an interest in everything imaginable; from Painting to Cooking, Music and Architecture.

His contribution to the interminable construction of Milan's cathedral, for example, is confirmation that he was an excellent Architect. It is a well-known fact that the 'Cathedral Works' was an ongoing building site for over four centuries, started a hundred years before Leonardo arrived in Milan and ending, with the completion of the façade, in Napoleon's time.

In 1487, Leonardo was paid to prepare drawings for the Dome's cladding of the cathedral. The dome cladding is the tower, in this case on an octagonal base, which in Gothic churches like Milan's cathedral, supports and externally replaces the traditional dome built over the intersection of the church's nave and transepts.

The problem of the dome cladding could not easily be solved and when Ludovico became Duke, it had already delayed the works for decades. Aware that Leonardo, Bramante and a few others were capable of solving the problem, Ludovico decided to have it solved once and for all. He commissioned plans from the five or six most prestigious names frequenting his court.

In 1490, wooden models of each dome cladding design were presented at the Duke's Castle. In the end, it was not Leonardo's design that was built, but that of Giovanni Antonio Amadeo (in reality, it was a synthesis of the best in each of the designs). The point is that the thirty-five-year-old Leonardo's reputation as an architect was such that the Duke had no hesitation in appointing him to design a literally 'central' part of the structure of the cathedral that is still today the fourth largest in Europe.

A year later, in 1488, Andrea del Verrocchio died.

Three years earlier he had moved to his studio in Venice to work on the gigantic equestrian monument to Bartolomeo Colleoni, which had been commissioned by the Venetian Republic.

Leonardo must have mourned his Master Verrocchio, with all the heartfelt sincerity that was his nature.

Ludovico Sforza also wanted at all costs to commemorate his father, Francesco, with an equestrian monument which would be the talk of all Europe and indeed, it was one of the projects for which he had asked Lorenzo de' Medici to send Leonardo to Milan.

In 1489, having grown impatient with the many projects that had been distracting the Florentine artist for the last seven years, Ludovico summoned him and pointed him in the right direction. Leonardo, bordering on insolence, as was his way, complained that he had never received a penny, but promised to start work and threw himself with renewed enthusiasm into his studies of anatomy, producing, among other things, some splendid drawings of human skulls, now kept in the Royal Collection at Windsor.

But amongst the countless activities which occupied Leonardo during what is known as his 'first Milanese period' and possibly the one that made him most famous and which was talked about and sought after by the crowned heads of Europe, was linked to the title of *Great Master of Revelries and Banquets* at the Sforza court. In practice, apart from the gastronomic aspect, which I will discuss later, this was the role of theatrical architect and inventor of shows for which, in the case of the Duke of Milan, *money was no object*. It should be explained that in the Renaissance, the families, and even more so, the courts, which aspired to gain prestige transformed every happy event. From a simple Birthday to a full reception, his projects put to work Tailors, Cooks, Musicians, Acrobats and Court Artists. These were occasions where no two costumes could be the same, since each model was specifically made to measure for the gentry.

The artists, including Leonardo, often took on duties they were not accustomed to, but they did so because these roles were well paid and allowed them to enjoy the privileges of the court.

So it was, that in 1490, at the end of his expansive Milanese 'career', Leonardo organized the celebrations for the wedding of Galeazzo Maria Sforza to Isabella of Aragon. Politically this was one of the most important marriages of a period, marked, as we shall see later, by the violent struggle between France and Spain for possession of a large part of Italy.

In the long season of banquets and other events (the wedding had been celebrated the previous year, but the death of the bride's mother had caused the festivities to be postponed), the *Feast of Paradise* stands out as the most lavish of all. It was held on 13 January at the Sforza Castle. With texts by the poet Bernardo Bellincioni and scenery by Leonardo (though some have said he also provided the music), the revelries went down in history as a perfect example of the mixture of luxury, erudition, decadence and creativity that distinguished the Italian Renaissance.

The hall where the celebration was held was at the top of the staircase by which horses could reach the castle, in front of Ludovico's private rooms, a long, narrow gallery with seven windows overlooking the courtyard and entrances to the ducal apartment.

Festoons of greenery bearing the Sforza and Aragon coats of arms hung from the ceiling, while the satin-covered walls displayed canvases recounting Francesco Sforza's achievements.

There was an imposing stage with steps leading up to it and another, lower down, for the musicians, high-backed chairs and benches for the counselors and dignitaries and, in the middle of the room, a carpeted 'court' for the Dukes. On the other side of the room was 'Paradise', concealed behind a curtain of satin.

It was here that the long and varied entertainment was performed, a theatrical event unique of its kind, which included allegories, dances, singing and acting.

In the words of the Este ambassador, Iacopo Trotti, who was present at the event:

"The following operetta composed by Messer Bernardo Belinzon [Bellincioni] for a performance called 'Paradise' was commissioned by Ludovico in honor of the Duchess of Milan; and it was called 'Paradise' since it was created by the masterly art of the Florentine, Master Leonardo da Vinci. 'Paradise', with all seven planets in movement, represented by men in splendid costumes and all these planets sang hymns of praise to the Duchess Isabella."

The revelry started in the late evening, after a musical prelude of pipes and trombones and a Neapolitan dance to the sound of tambourines, in which Isabella herself took part: *"She was beautiful and innocent and shone like the sun"* commented Trotti. The Duchess was then presented with mock 'diplomatic missions', which were an excuse to introduce Spanish, Polish, Hungarian, Turkish, German and French dances and masquerades.

Then the curtain fell and a Boy-Angel announced the celebration (as in Florentine sacred plays). After a short concert, Jupiter spoke in praise of Isabella and held a dialogue with Apollo, who marveled at the existence of a new sun capable of blinding him. Then the planets descended from their places and went to sit on a mountaintop (in other words, they came down from heaven to earth); Mercury went to Isabella to announce the descent of Jupiter and the gift of three graces and the seven virtues; each planet decided on a gift for Isabella and Apollo delivered them to the Duchess, together with a 'booklet' containing all the words recited in the play.

A novelty in this spectacle, talked of long afterwards, was what today we would call 'special effects'; a large machine invented by Leonardo suddenly appeared to the spectators in the darkness, causing them to cry out in surprise at the lights passing through openings and window panes, creating plays of shadows on the walls, in a *crescendo* of vocal, instrumental and visual harmonies.

The following is taken from another report of that period:

"'Paradise' was represented as a sort of half egg, with the interior completely gilded and full of lights representing the stars and at different levels were placed the planets, men in costumes, who sang and played instruments. Around the upper edge of the egg were arranged the twelve signs of the Zodiac and each of these carried in their hands glass spheres containing lights, extremely beautiful to see, and this heavenly scene was accompanied by sweet singing and gentle

music."

Those present were so fascinated by these revelries that they were soon imitated in Genoa in November of the same year, on the occasion of the wedding of Eleonora Sanseverino and Giovanni Adorno. To all effects, it was a consecration by the Florentine genius. Until now we have spoken mostly about the 'technical' aspects of Leonardo's work, but not everyone knows that he was also a forerunner of environmentalists, and demonstrated showing in this too, that he was capable of predicting the future, or rather, of guessing the consequences of the often mistaken actions of humans regarding the planet.

Leonardo did not believe that people were fundamentally good, indeed, some people did not seem to him to be worthy even of the bodies that nature had given them. In some of his notebooks on the study of muscles, we read:

"I do not believe that men of low habits, those that are hostile and that speak little, deserve to inhabit such perfect machines. Since their nature makes them inclined to eating and drinking, to mediocrity and evil, it does not lead them to appreciate others or themselves and so they gradually destroy themselves as well as everything that surrounds them."

Still on the subject of the human species:

"Animals (men) will be seen on the earth who are always fighting among themselves, causing great damage and death on both sides. And all this will never end since man is the

most savage of the animals. Because of man, whole forests will be destroyed and he will be capable of annihilating everything natural that remains. Oh planet earth! Why do you not open up and swallow these evil beings into the depths of your entrails and never show the heavens again such cruel and merciless monsters?"

And yet again:

"Due to the stupidities and acts of madness committed by man, the world will move on toward its end."

It really seems that we are listening to / reading a news reporter of our own time. More than a philosopher – a qualification no-one has ever denied him – here it would be appropriate to speak of Leonardo as a prophet!

At a certain point, in fact, he started to write a series of apparently irrational texts that were linked to the terrifying prophecies that were widespread in those years, such as, for example, the sermons and threats of Savonarola, the Dominican friar, against the moral corruption of Rome under the Borgias.

These 'prophecies' had to be declaimed, as Leonardo writes, *"in a form of frenzy or delirium, insanity of the brain"*. The prophet who declaimed them must have appeared to be in a state of fever of the senses and fantasy, delirium or hallucination, a similar condition to that traditionally associated with Sibyls and Priestesses of the Oracle.

Only recently has it been discovered that this was only a long chain of riddles, whose solutions were to be considered funny. The most terrifying scenes dissolved into the most common objects and situations of daily life.

Here is a macabre and dark example which seems to refer to the resurrection of the dead:

"We will see the bones of the dead, moving fast, and decide on the fate of those who made them move."

In short, this seems to be a vision of the Prophet Ezekiel's 'Valley of Bones', when in fact it is only a riddle, the answer to which is Dice, which at that time were made of bone.

So Leonardo delighted in conjuring, rhymes, allegories, jokes and puzzles (including some which are still unsolved). It was recounted that at court revelries he usually left the guests dumbfounded by making differently colored flames burst from a bowl of boiling water, just by throwing some red wine into it. Or he would challenge his table companions to break with a single blow a wooden stick balanced between two glass goblets full to the brim with wine, without making the goblets fall or the wine spill. As a student of the chemical transformation of substances and the laws of physics, he did not find these tricks particularly difficult, but in the eyes of the public, what he was able to invent was a cause for genuine amazement. It is no coincidence that he was accused several times of practicing demoniac rites, just because they were not able to explain certain 'devilish inventions'.

Like anyone, outside the normal run of things, Leonardo was either greatly loved or greatly hated. Despite everything, the members of the court and the Duke himself loved to spend time talking to him. He was considered wise and erudite and children loved his stories.

These were tales he invented himself, but not the usual fanciful or chivalrous poems; they were simple fables, some short, others longer, but always with a precise moral, aimed at understanding the important things in life.

Here are some examples:

The pebble:
"A beautiful, shiny, hard pebble lay amidst the grass and colorful flowers at the edge of a quiet wood, along which ran a pathway that was also made of pebbles. Seeing all these pebbles similar to herself, the pebble thought: "Oh, if only I could roll along among my friends! What am I doing here surrounded by this silent, boring grass?"

So, by pushing herself hard, she rolled down and ended up on the path amidst many, anonymous pebbles. But she immediately realized her mistake, since every passing cart crushed her, every horseshoe splintered her, not to mention the dung dropped by the animals passing there, which she had no way of avoiding.

She spent the rest of her days in this way, unable to return to the tranquil spot she had left. The same fate awaits those who leave the contemplative solitude of the countryside and become mixed up in the chaos of the cities, infested by the worst type of people and ways of thinking."

The falcon and the duck:
"A falcon who could not wait for his prey, a duck, to re-emerge from the water, dived straight into the pond, under the illusion that he could catch the duck immediately. But he had not thought that his feathers, made heavy by the water, would prevent him rising in flight. So it happened that while

the duck flew away in perfect tranquility, the falcon had to struggle not to drown."

The flame and the candle:
"Once upon a time, there was a fireplace where a large quantity of wood burned, so much that there was enough to provide heat for at least two days. The flames burned and danced about with pleasure, enjoying each others' company and their laughter resounded in continual crackling.

Now it happened that someone put near the fireplace a beautiful silver candelabra with as yet unlit candles in it, so pure and "appetizing" for the fire. So it was that a rebellious flame leapt away from her sisters and went to light the wick of the candle, which immediately lit.

But, alas, the life of a candle is short and short too was the life of the flame, which quickly went out in a mist of unpleasant smoke. She would have liked to go back and live a little longer with her sisters, but her voracity led to her ruin."

I have mentioned earlier the culinary aspect of Leonardo's role as 'Master of the Banquets'. An ironical and disenchanted testimony is provided by Sabba da Castiglione, the Florentine Ambassador to Milan, who spied on Leonardo and in his monthly report to the Signoria informed them what the genius from Vinci was getting up to at the Sforza Castle:

"Master Leonardo's kitchen is a shambles... now, instead of twenty cooks previously busy over the stoves, there are more than two hundred people wandering about and I have seen none of them do any cooking, they just busy themselves *with these large machines that occupy the walls and floors..."*

Among the gadgets that refused to work, were a beef-grinder worked by horses, an automatic roasting spit worked by the hot air from the oven and a wind-driven bread-cutter. In the middle of cog wheels, gears, pulleys and infuriated cooks, Leonardo was a bungling gourmet chef, passionate about simple dishes that were catastrophically complicated to prepare.

Leonardo's passion for cooking is well known and it is strange that he never wrote about it.

We know that his father, Ser Piero, had married Caterina to a retired pastry cook of Vinci, Accatabriga di Piero del Vacca, who had taught the young Leonardo the secrets of culinary art.

We also know that he had met the apprentice Sandro Botticelli at Verrocchio's studio, and years later the two opened a tavern, *The Three Frogs* of Sandro and Leonardo (the idea that two of the greatest artists of the Italian Renaissance had worked together as cooks and restaurant owners has something deliciously Italian about it).

But before this experience with Botticelli, in order to earn some money, Leonardo had worked as a waiter at the *Tavern of the Three Snails* on the Ponte Vecchio. When the three cooks died, mysteriously poisoned, he stepped in as chef (improbable as it may seem, the story is absolutely true).

It seems, however, that the customers were not very appreciative of his attempts to modernize the menu with a kind of 'nouvelle cuisine' based on artistically sculpted vegetables and mini-portions that were absolutely anachronistic in a period where sumptuous banquets were in vogue. Some of the dishes on Leonardo's menu were: "*two half cucumbers on a leaf of lettuce*", "*a beautifully engraved carrot*", "*a frog's leg on a dandelion leaf*", "*a roulade of anchovy atop a round of turnip sculpted in the style of a frog*". Once again, Leonardo was centuries ahead of his contemporaries. But Leonardo's most creative years in the kitchen were those at Ludovico's court where he was the Great Master of Revelries and Banquets.

There he was immediately removed from responsibility for the menus (he was now a declared vegetarian, while a typical Court banquet would include 600 sausages, 300 stuffed pigs' trotters, 200 calves, 60 peacocks, etc. etc.), but he made up for it by inventing the machines of every kind seen by the Florentine Ambassador, which he had intended to be used to lighten the heavier work in the kitchen: the roaster, the steam water heater, the grinder, the wind-driven bread cutter, the ventilator, the garlic crusher, the pepper grinder, the nut crackers worked by three horses, the corkscrew for left-handed users, an egg-cutter and the gigantic watercress-slicer.

On its first demonstration, this last device unhappily caused the death of six laborers and three gardeners. Ludovico successfully used a modified version of it in battle.

Incredibly, between one disaster and another, almost reluctant to give up his 'toys', Leonardo found time to paint such works as *The Lady with an Ermine* and *The Last Supper*.

VI

I had started off with the bread rolls and now hands had appeared.

The symbolism of that parallel will escape no-one, even those who are not Catholic or are not familiar with the Eucharist. After all, the sacred nature of breaking bread is recognized by all religions, all cultures. It immediately seemed to me to be a veiled allusion to the universalistic thought of Leonardo, but then I realized that it was more probably another example of his 'Jewish' reading of the Gospels.

Leonardo was aware of the 'Jewishness' of Jesus, as almost all Christians are nowadays, but in his time, the Church did not emphasize the Jewish origin of the majority of the acts performed by Jesus and the Apostles. All feast-day meals in Jewish households start with the ritual blessing of the wine and the bread. Even if in inverse order, this is the origin of the Eucharistic rite instituted by Jesus during *The Last Supper*, as recounted by Luke in chapter 22 of his

Gospel:

"And he took bread, and gave thanks, and brake it, and gave unto them, saying, This is my body which is given for you: this do in remembrance of me. Likewise also the cup after supper, saying, This cup is the new testament in my blood, which is shed for you."

Those two small words, 'gave thanks', which pass almost unnoticed, are the demonstration that this was a Jewish supper, that the rite performed by those at the table was Jewish. Then, however, come the words, *"this do in remembrance of me"*, from which Christianity drew the *new* ritual of the Eucharist. Now the bread represents the body of Christ and certainly needs no other justification to figure as part of the enigma that Leonardo was concealing in the painting. However, hands in the *Holy Scri*pture, are for blessing, consecrating, baptizing, oiling, giving or returning life and healing. In fact, the role of hands in the life of a priest is really fundamental. In the celebration of the Eucharist, according to the Roman canon, at the moment of the consecration, the priest says these words:

"On the day before His Passion, He took bread in his holy, venerable hands ...broke the bread, gave it to his disciples saying... after the supper, taking also this magnificent chalice in his holy venerable hands, giving thanks in like manner ... gave it to his disciples, saying..."

Bread and hands, bread and hands...
It must also be said, for the sake of completeness and

intellectual honesty, that if Leonardo based *The Last Supper* on St. John's *Gospel* and I am convinced that he did, then the institution of the Eucharist (*"do this in remembrance of me"*), does not in fact appear in this *Gospel*. Many have noted the absence of a chalice on the table laid by Leonardo. Yes, there are tiny wine goblets, but the Holy Grail is not there, there is no 'magnificent chalice' of the Catholic liturgy. The best possible explanation for this is that it is missing because John did not record these phrases, and Leonardo was following John's description of the supper to the letter.

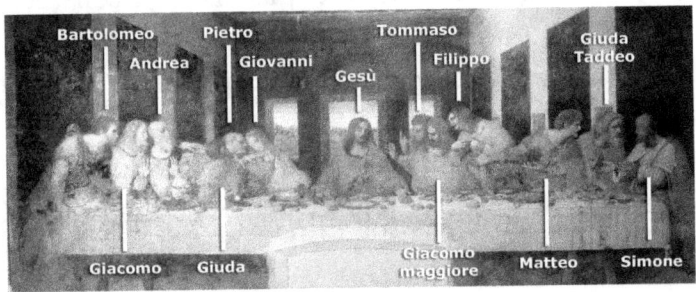

[English names L-R Bartholomew, James, Andrew, Judas, Peter, John, Jesus, Thomas, James the Greater, Philip, Matthew, Jude Thaddeus, Simon]

Despite this inconsistency, the more I thought about it, the more I felt convinced that Leonardo had given the bread and hands not only a deep significance linked to the Eucharist, but had also provided a clue that would allow me to identify the hidden traces of the music.

I felt as if I were on a threshold and that once I had stepped over it, the solution to the enigma would appear in all its simplicity and elegance.

Of course, my first thought was to read the hands as musical notes, as I had done with the bread rolls. But despite the overpowering desire to place black balls also on the hands and to try to play 'bread rolls and hands together', I decided to dwell on the odd sensation I had experienced with Andrew's hands: as if the Apostles' hands and gestures were providing also indications of the movement of the secret music.

It was as if the Apostles, with the rhythmic and sinuous movements of their hands, were making me understand which direction the melody should take, they were simply accompanying it with their gestures.

Or, to put it differently, it was as if Leonardo had entrusted to the hands of each Apostle in the sequence, the role of an orchestral conductor's hands for that 'little piece' of music.

Starting from the right and leaving aside the bread rolls for a moment on the table, I started to note the sequence of the gestures:

- The first Apostle, Simon the Zealot, holds his hands up midway in the air, his palms turned upwards;

- The second Apostle, Jude Thaddeus, holds his right hand turned toward himself with the fingers upwards and almost in line with Simon's hands, while the left hand is placed on the table;

- The third Apostle from the right, Matthew, is making a broad gesture that seems to indicate Jesus with both hands, these too more or less aligned with Simon's; Mathew's right hand, the hand closest to Jesus, ends up being directly beneath those of Philip;

- The fourth Apostle, Philip, is bringing both hands towards his chest, in a gesture that seems to say: "*Who, me?*" – an impression confirmed by his agonized expression;

- The fifth Apostle, James the Greater, has spread his hands open in horror, the right hand almost touching Jesus (although, it is clear from his face, this was not the Apostle's intention), while the left, just above the table, is almost exactly under Matthew's right hand and Philip's left;

- The sixth and last Apostle of those on Jesus' left, Thomas, has his right forefinger raised, almost showing it to Jesus, a mysterious gesture with many esoteric interpretations (in his portrait of the prophet in the desert, for example, Leonardo also represents John the Baptist with the right forefinger raised).

I also made a brief note of the connection, certainly not casual, between the hands and the bread rolls on the table. For example, there is bread placed at right angles below the left hands (why always the left, I wonder?) of Simon, Matthew and Philip.

Moving over to the left side of the painting, to the Apostles on Jesus' right, the first thing I noted was the grouping of hands placed on the table; Jesus' right hand, the apparently crossed hands of John and the left hand of Judas Iscariot seem almost to be touching.

- Following this incongruous group of four hands, is the left hand of Peter, which, although it seems to be placed on the shoulder of the 'favorite disciple', John, in order to attract his attention, it is placed sideways in front of the neck of the other Apostle and could also possibly be a threatening allusion to his beheading.

- Then comes the right hand of Judas, holding the bag of money tightly. As soon as I first noted the positions and movements of the hands, I had a distinct feeling that the hand of the betrayer would not form part of the melody. Judas, the outcast, who had distanced himself from Jesus, is represented by Leonardo in an area of shade, a sort of inner isolation. The play of light and colors, his position in the foreground, as if he were leaning towards the observer of the painting, alienates him from everything that is happening around him.

- After Judas' right hand, comes the left hand of James, whose arm is stretched out behind the Apostle Andrew to touch Peter's shoulder, as if he wanted to intervene in what Peter is asking John. Here too, as in the cases of Simon, Matthew and Philip, there seems to be a flow, a movement passing from one Apostle to another. James touches the shoulder of Peter, who is touching the shoulder of John, like runners passing a baton.

- Directly beneath James' left hand is the mysterious hand with the knife, the hand that does not seem to belong to any of the figures in the painting. Some maintain that during one of the attempts to restore the fresco – which, as we know, started to have problems with its adhesion to the wall while Leonardo was still alive – someone had actually made a modification in order to make that hand 'anatomically plausible'.

In any case, the consensus of expert opinion is that, despite the wrist being bent at a problematic angle, it is the right hand of Peter who, later the same night, with that same knife, would cut off the ear of the servant of the high priest of the temple.

- Then come Andrew's hands, whose open palms towards the observer we had already noted in the previous chapter, meaning either his disassociation from Jesus' accusation, or a slowing down of the musical phrase.

- James' right hand does not appear and must presumably be under the edge of the table, which, in fact, can be seen between his right elbow and Bartholomew's left hand.

- Finally, Bartholomew's hands, both placed on the table, with the right hand, as we have already seen, immediately adjacent to the last bread roll, meaning the last note, the end of the musical phrase.

Here too, as in the case of the Apostles on Jesus' left, I made notes on the connection between hands and bread and here too I found strange coincidences; a bread roll next to the right hand of Jesus, one next to Judas' bag, one exactly underneath Andrew's hands and one, already mentioned, adjacent to Bartholomew's hand.

Again, at least three of these bread rolls are located precisely above the same number of 'folds' in the tablecloth. I had confirmation, therefore, of the link between the Apostles' hands and the bread rolls arranged in the foreground of the table.

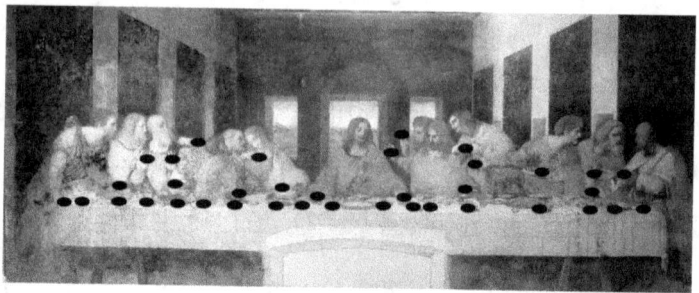

In order finally to make the notes, I superimposed the black balls not only over the bread rolls, but this time, also over the hands. But, I was still missing something. Since I had understood that the hands were the second factor in the enigma, the idea of the centrality of the number three both in the visible painting and in the musical enigma was haunting me, forcing me to look for a third factor to complete the triad. I finally identified it as the first goblet placed at the extreme right of the table.

The third factor must be the wine, since this would create the symbolic triad of *wine* (the Blood of Christ), *bread* (the Body of Christ) and *hands* (the instruments of consecration and distribution of the Eucharist). To this third factor, the goblet of wine, I attributed the role of the sign that would start the phrase of music. I was ready to transcribe the black dots onto a score, ready to try once more to play the symbols I had found, but thinking of the score reminded me of a detail that did not answer, a further knot to be untied. If what I had identified as possible musical notes were either on or above the table (the Apostles' hands), then what was the role of the white space I had started from, the vertical part of the tablecloth with its vertical and horizontal folds, which made it look like an empty score?

Perhaps there was something wrong with the way I had approached that part of the research. I began feverishly to measure distances and proportions all over the place and soon discovered a coincidence that could provide me with the answer I was looking for. The height of the vertical part of the tablecloth was equal to the distance between the table and the raised forefinger of the Apostle on Jesus' left side, Thomas. I immediately realized where I had gone wrong. The tablecloth was not the score, it was only an allusion to a presence. As in all enigmas, it was as if Leonardo had wanted to test us all, saying:

"I am leaving you a clue, a score without music ... it is up to you to find the notes!"

The 'empty' score that was the tablecloth, needed to be *reversed* onto the scene above the table, where the notes were. I started to examine Thomas's raised forefinger, then again the base of the painting. My gaze passed quickly from one to the other until, suddenly, it all fell into place. Thomas's raised finger was the 'peak' of the composition, the line of bread rolls was the lowest point.

I had established two imaginary lines, the first and the last. The rectangular space between the two enclosed all the musical elements I was looking for.

I took a ruler and pencil and drew two horizontal lines. the first passed through the bread rolls along the base, in other words, the foreground edge of the table; and the second, parallel to the first, I drew to match the highest point, as marked by Thomas's forefinger. The next step was very simple. I had created two equal distances, the tablecloth below and the 'score' above. To obtain a stave, I only had to draw three more parallel lines equidistant from the two already drawn – three lines that would divide the score into four equal spaces.

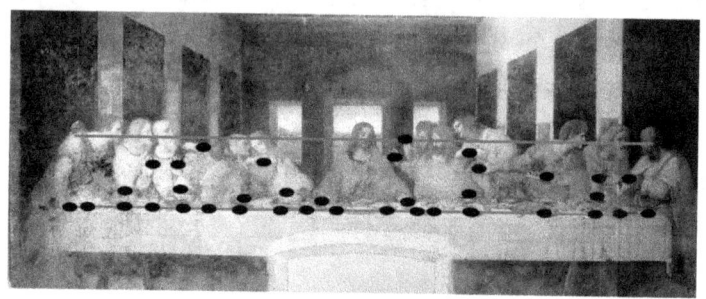

There, now I had it in front of me. It was the stave of *The Last Supper,* and the hands of the Apostles were placed in the spaces and on the lines, like swallows perching on wires suspended in the air; some close, other distant and solitary. In the same way, the bread rolls rested in their spaces. At last it all worked out. The music that had been silent since the day Leonardo's brilliant mind had created it was about to make the air vibrate. I was very moved and could not wait to play the music, but at the same time I wanted to savor the profound significance of my discovery.

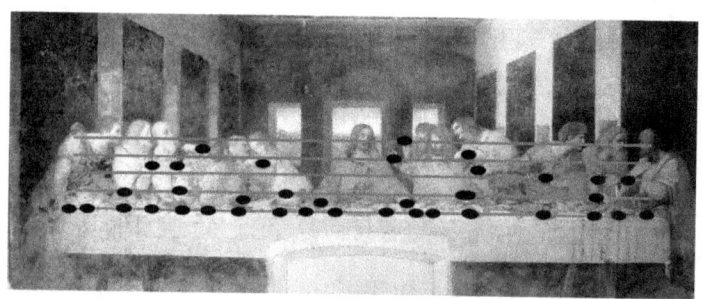

I was reminded of university studies I had undertaken years earlier on the philosophy of St. Augustine. In his treatise, *De Musica,* the Bishop of Hippo Regius stated that beauty in this world is the reflection of divine perfections that are found in music and harmonies, since it is in music that its greatest expression is achieved. All at once, while I was recovering from the excitement of the discovery, I realized that the last upper line I had drawn and the line drawn through Thomas's forefinger, touched the ears of almost all the Apostles, as well as those of Jesus.

The forefinger and the ears. I froze.

It was as if Leonardo was saying:

"Listen to me, you who are looking... do not use only your sight, use all your senses..."

VII

In 1492, Christopher Columbus discovered America. This was an event of such importance that some historians chose that year to mark the watershed between two epochs, the Middle Ages and Modernity. It is no longer considered appropriate to divide history into such defined periods as to give precise dates to their beginning and end, but there is no doubt that the end of the fourteenth century was a time of significant changes and that their consequences still affect us today.

It is no coincidence that 1492 falls exactly in the middle of the hundred years from Johannes Gutenberg's invention of the printing press (1447) to the publication by Nicholas Copernicus (1542) of the *De revolutionibus orbium coelestium*, a hundred years, which, by all accounts, did bring the Middle Ages to an end and gave new birth to the modern era. But 1492 was not only the year of Columbus' discovery. Six months earlier, in April, Lorenzo the Magnificent met his untimely death (at only 43 years of age), probably due to an ulcer (even if his contemporaries spoke of gout), which the best physicians of the age did not know how to cure.

His death destabilized the situation in Italy to such an extent that two years later it hastened the invasion by Charles VIII of France.

In addition, in July, three months after Lorenzo – Innocent VIII, the Genovese Pope also died. Poisoned by Rodrigo Borgia, so it was said. The noble Spaniard Borgia took the papal throne under the name of Alexander VI and the following year, upon Columbus's return, hurriedly allocated the New World to the Spanish Crown.

In short, 1492 was by no means any old year and where was Leonardo while all this was happening? He was taking a long trip as a 'tourist', we would say today, around the Alps in Lombardy. He visited Lake Como, Valtellina, Valsassina, Valchiavenna, Bellagio. He sketched the mountains, took the baths at Sondrio (the hostelry where he stayed still exists and is extremely proud of this fact) and in general celebrated his fortieth birthday in his usual style, feverishly curious and a lover of the beauty and pleasures of life.

One of his travel notes says:

"Voltolina (Valtellina), as it is called, a valley surrounded by high and terrible mountains, makes many strong wines and raises so many cattle that the country folk conclude they produce more milk than wine."

In 1493, a woman named Caterina came to live with Leonardo in Milan. Even if some historians are not certain that this was his mother, there are notes stating that he had invited her to come; there is also the fact that at the time it was usual for a widow (and Accatabriga da Vinci had just died) to go and live with one of her children, and finally, it appears that this Caterina died shortly afterwards, which would be compatible with his mother's age.

Some say that Leonardo spent only a modest amount on the funeral, but this could be explained by his long-standing reluctance to divulge the circumstances of his birth, these being circumstances that Leonardo would have felt were lacking in respect to his mother's memory.

In the same year that Caterina arrived – something that must have worked miracles on the artist's humor and morale – Leonardo presented the Duke with a clay model of the horse for the equestrian monument to his father. Unfortunately, the bronze smelting of the statue attempted the year after was a failure. Now that Charles VIII's invasion of Italy had already begun, the Moor decided to send the tons of bronze intended for the equestrian statue to Ferrara for the making of canons. Despite this disappointment, relations between the two remained good and 1494 was also the year in which Ludovico commissioned Leonardo to paint the fresco at Santa Maria delle Grazie. In fact, the heraldic crests appearing on the arches above the ceiling of the room where *The Last Supper* was painted are those of the Sforza family, which indicates that it was the Duke, and not the Dominicans of the monastery, who commissioned the work.

Leonardo started painting in the following year, 1495, probably because of the events of 1494, including the expulsion of the Medici from a Florence that had fallen into the hands of the King of France and which offered too little future security for an artist to undertake such a long and demanding project. Without going into the details of this incredibly complex political situation, it is nevertheless appropriate to say that in the last decade of the fifteenth century, reversals of power, betrayals and alliances of convenience made the choices of 'Court Artists', in Italy, very difficult and risky. Putting into practice an Italian travesty that would delay national unity for almost four centuries, Ludovico invited Charles VIII to take up the French monarchy's claims on the kingdom of Naples.

He did so in order to protect his own duchy from the sights of Ferdinand I of Aragon, but he regretted it when, four years later, Charles' heir, Louis XII, invaded Italy again and entered Milan, forcing Ludovico to take refuge with Maximilian I of Habsburg, Holy Roman Emperor (This caused Leonardo to seek safety in Mantua, the following year).

The interesting aspect of this 'see-saw' of power, from the viewpoint of the life and works of Leonardo, is the ability of the French to invade Italy just when and how they wished, conquering prosperous and important cities almost without striking a blow, thanks to their winning weapon, their revolutionary artillery. No historian would dream of denying that war is the most important driving force behind the technological progress of every period. From the Copper, Bronze and Iron Ages to the invention of gunpowder and on to the twentieth century, with its Airplanes, Submarines, Radar and the Atomic Bomb, there has never been a scientific discovery that has not been wanted, financed and immediately exploited by the 'Warlords' of every era.

Gunpowder had been known since the thirteenth century and starting from two hundred years before Leonardo, we can already read of Bombards, Flintlocks and other examples of rudimentary firearms. Despite this, halfway through the fifteenth century, wars were still won in battles where the real protagonists were archers and cavalry, and an army's most effective weapon was the crossbow – both handheld and mounted on carts.

In the years that Leonardo was working in Florence, canons started to fire balls of iron instead of stone, and everything changed. The high medieval walls, built to defend against catapults, arrows and assault towers, were totally unsuited to the new threat. A well-placed canon shot would make the wall crash down onto its defenders. Charles invested a great deal of money in this new artillery whose reputation, when it appeared on the other side of the Alps, was enough to open the gates of any city whose walls could not resist the French canons.

This also concerned Leonardo the architect.

Particularly, ten years later when he entered the service of Cesare Borgia, the son of Rodrigo (yes, in that period popes had children and at times even treated the Throne of St. Peter as if it were a 'Lordship' or Royalty; something to be bequeathed).

Leonardo was in fact one of the first to design *modern style* fortifications, with square or pentagonal bastions instead of towers and with walls that were very thick and tapering, so that if a cannonball struck a buttress that was several meters thick and had a sloping surface, it could damage it, but certainly not cause it to collapse.

This short interlude on military history was only necessary to point out that the years in which Leonardo was working on *The Last Supper*, from 1495 to 1497, were dangerous years, full of fear and uncertainty for everyone.

On one day, news would arrive of the victory over Charles VIII at Fornovo by the Sforza and the Gonzaga families, allied with Venice. On another day, it became known that Savonarola – the Dominican preacher, who, after the Medici rule had been thrown out, set up a strange puritan and mystical "republic" in Florence and had rebelled against the Pope, resulting in his excommunication. To Leonardo's great grief, on yet another day, the death of Beatrice d'Este was announced. In the midst of all this, Leonardo rushed from one project to another, almost as if he felt that time was getting short, as is described very realistically by his friend, the short-story writer, Matteo Bandello:

"I often saw him, early in the morning, climb up the scaffolding, because The Last Supper is very high up from the ground; usually he did not put his brush down from when the sun rose until late in the evening, forgetting even to eat and drink, and painting continuously. Then, two, three or even four days would pass without him touching it again, but spending one or two hours a day simply contemplating it, examining it, debating over it with himself and judging the figures. I also saw him (according to how the whim or fancy took him) at midday, in high summer, leave the Old Court, where he went to sculpt that amazing clay horse, coming straight to the Grazie and up on the scaffolding, take his brush, make one or two strokes to one of the figures and then immediately leave again and go somewhere else."

This is an amazing 'portrait' not only of the restless Leonardo, but of true artists of all time, who are forced by a sudden inspiration to abandon one activity, probably the one that is providing them with their livelihood, to run to paint or write, or play – the idea that has just formed in their feverish minds.

Those who saw *The Last Supper* when it was just completed were overcome by the revolutionary way in which it broke the mould no less than by the beauty of the painting itself (Vasari defined it 'a very beautiful and marvelous thing'*)*. In fact, and it is a mystery that he managed to avoid being censured by the Dominican friars, Leonardo had introduced new ideas that were provocative, to say the least.

For example, neither Christ nor the Holy Apostles have a halo, an attribute born of Byzantine iconography but affirmed in all Christian art which had become, by this time, practically obligatory. Some critics noted that the window behind Jesus, thanks to the artist's brilliant use of light, gives Christ a 'natural' halo, which could have silenced any objections by the friars.

In reality, Leonardo simply found these artificial gilded circles unnatural and superfluous.

There is worse, however.

All the paintings of the Last Supper before this one, placed Judas clearly outside the 'brotherhood' of the Apostles or had him sit on the other side of the table from them or even showed him already in the process of leaving the room in order to go and denounce Jesus to the Temple priests.

Leonardo, however, even if the light on Judas is different and his body is leaning further forward than the others, gave him a position of equal dignity. He is at Jesus' table with the other eleven, his bag held tightly in his hand, and this, much more than the absence of the haloes, must have caused considerable perplexity among the theologians of Santa Maria. Nevertheless, in this case too, Leonardo did things his own way.

Then there is the thesis of the Apostle in whom Leonardo painted his own portrait; many believe this to be Jude Thaddeus. The habit of certain artists to insert their own portrait into their works as a signature was effectively already known in the Renaissance period, even if it would be Caravaggio, a hundred years later, who made it widespread to the point of becoming fashionable. Now, the thesis of some (to my mind too radical), is that Leonardo chose Jude Thaddeus, whose physical appearance (long hair, long beard) recalls that of the artist, because he was the only Apostle who *had his back turned to Jesus.* This could confirm that Leonardo belonged to the secret congregations of Gnostic heretics, who denied Jesus' divinity.

First of all, it should be said that Matthew too had his back turned to Jesus, caught up as he is, together with Jude Thaddeus, in a discussion with Simon. And how can it be maintained that Jude Thaddeus' long, white beard and hair are similar to those of Leonardo when the artist was only 43 years old when he started the painting?

We have no portraits of Leonardo at that age, but it seems to me somewhat improbable that he already resembled the Leonardo of the famous self-portrait as an old man.

The Last Supper, as is well known, is not technically a 'fresco'. The name fresco comes from the fact that the color was applied to plaster that was still fresh and was done very quickly and before the plaster could dry, so that the amalgam of background and color, which gave the fresco its incredible resistance to the attacks of climate and weather, could be achieved.

But as we have just seen, Leonardo liked to stop work, contemplate what he had done and change his ideas on how to depict something or somebody.

In short, he liked painting on a wall in the same way as he painted on board or canvas and in the case of *The Last Supper* he used an oily tempera made of linseed oil and egg, spread over a double layer of plaster.

Unfortunately, the use of organic materials and the unsuitable environmental circumstances of the refectory soon caused the work to deteriorate, as already cited by Vasari in his work '*Lives*'.

The first attempt at restoration took place two years before Leonardo's death in 1517 and contributed, like all those that followed over the centuries, to making things worse.

Only since 1999, and let us hope it continues to be true, does the last restoration seem to have stopped the deterioration of the surface – and revealed, for the first time since the work was completed by Leonardo, many details that had disappeared, such as, the decoration of some drapes on the walls of the room and various objects on the table.

Few people were more grateful than me for the reappearance of those 'objects', and in the forthcoming chapters you will understand why.

VIII

I had found the stave of *The Last Supper*.

But if Leonardo had hidden music in *The Last Supper* – and by now I was sure he had – how could I be equally sure that he had done so by using the same musical notation – the stave, in fact – that a modern musician would use?

Well, the answer is that the stave had already existed for several centuries. Moreover, in the musical phrase from the Windsor Codex shown in a previous chapter, we have proof that Leonardo too was familiar with it.

Despite the simplicity of this answer, I would like to give a brief overview of the medieval chapter of the history of music and conclude it with evidence of the presence of an organ in the church of Santa Maria delle Grazie while Leonardo worked on the fresco, another concrete clue supporting the thesis that he painted a musical enigma on the refectory wall. Without going back too far into time, the first system of writing music – in reality, it was little more than a way of indicating to the singers the different heights of the notes they had to reach and was created in the eleventh century by the Benedictine monk Guido d'Arezzo (992-1050). This is called today *Diastematic Notation* and was used almost only as a reminder of the ascending or descending melodic line in Gregorian chants.

Guido d'Arezzo named his system a *Tetragram*, because he had inserted signs, called *Neumes* (the modern notes), into a sort of grid made up of four parallel lines and, consequently, three spaces. The notes were graphically represented by squares, which subsequently took on a rhomboid shape and then finally became round. These notes, positioned either on the lines or in the spaces, were allocated names by d'Arezzo according to the initial syllable of the first six verses of the Latin hymn to St. John, protector of singers:

ut (UT queant laxis), which in the seventeenth century took the name of *do*, named after musicologist Giovanni Battista Doni (do comes from DOni);
re (REsonare fibris);
mi (MIra gestorum);
fa (FAmuli tuorum);
sol (SOLve polluti), now called *so* in English;
la (LAbii reatum) and finally;
sj (The initials of *S*ancte *J*ohannes) which in the sixteenth century was written definitively in Italian as *si*, now called *ti* in English.

To this memorization technique, d'Arezzo gave the name of *solmization* (from sol-mi).

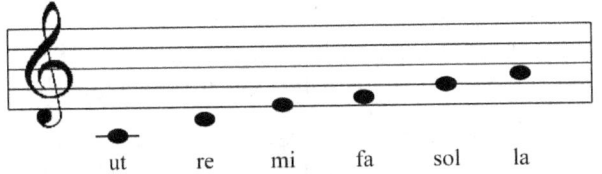

An example of Guido d'Arezzo's natural hexachord.

In the following decades, the technical requirements linked to reading music caused Guido d'Arezzo's Tetragram, with four lines and three spaces, to evolve into a version with five lines and four spaces, which took on its present name of Pentagram and was already known and widely used during the Renaissance.

Only in 1260 did Francone di Colonia introduce the duration figures of the notes, thus adjusting the writing of music to precise mathematical criteria.

The musical figures used in the Renaissance were the following:

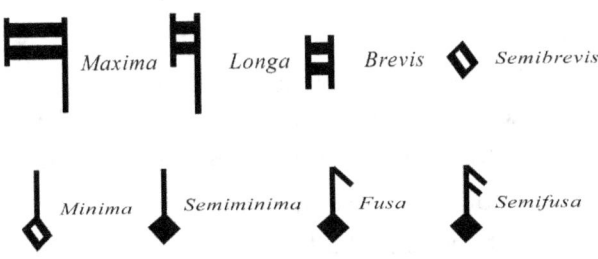

The eight figures used in the Renaissance

The melody (or sung line) was written using a Clef that in the following centuries became the G Clef, or Treble Clef, also called the 'Violin clef'. Music from the Middle Ages until the Renaissance was 'Modal', in the sense that each composition implied the choice of a mode, that is of a scale. There were eight modes of Benedictine origin, divided into four 'Authentic' modes (Doric, Phrygian, Lydian, Mixolydian) and four 'Plagal' modes (Hypodoric, Hypophrygian, Hypolydian, Hypomixolydian). After the fifteenth century, music became 'stably tonal', in other words, in order to compose, an intonation sound had to be identified, called the 'Tonic' or the first degree of a major or minor scale, around which the scale was then constructed.

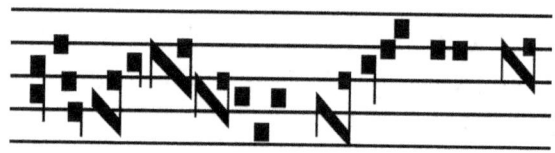

Notation used in a fourteenth century Gregorian chant.

In the Renaissance, as we saw with the *Feast of Paradise*, court festivities, tournaments and jousts were created in grand style in order to disseminate an image of the power of the cities and their lords. Music played a fundamental role in these Arcadian scenarios.

In the Italian courts, a meeting point for European musicians and singers and the beating heart of the musical culture of the Renaissance Period, music accompanied all of the most important events, from public and private ceremonies to banquets of all kinds.

It had become fashionable to have artists present at court and the Lords competed with each other to have the best of these in their service, as they were considered symbols of Power, Culture, Prestige and Wealth (taking into account 'cultural proportions', it may be said that this is still a widespread fashion today).

In this sense, Italian courts were among the most splendid and lively; just think of the Medici in Florence, the Visconti and the Sforza in Milan, the Estensi in Ferrara or the Gonzaga in Mantua. The Lords' luxurious palazzi had special 'music rooms', set up for the mending of musical instruments and for performers and singers, who were held in high consideration and paid generously; often called in especially from other countries.

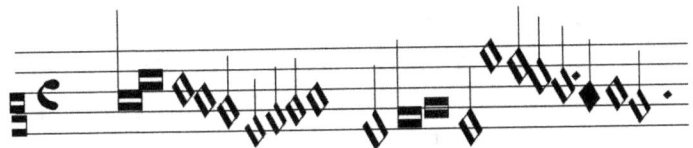

Musical phrase from the *missa "Au travail suis"* by Johannes Ockeghem.

The period 1474-1519, which coincided with Leonardo's adult years, was dominated both in music teaching and in the music world in general, by illustrious Flemish Masters. Among the most important of these were Guillaume Dufay, Josquin Desprez and above all Johannes Ockeghem, who died around 1497. Ockeghem was the First Choir Master at the French court, later becoming also Treasurer of the Cathedral of St. Martin de Tours. He is considered one of the fathers of Renaissance music, even though only a very small part of his production has survived, including; beautiful Motets, a few Masses and around twenty Secular songs.

In the Renaissance, there was a strict distinction between 'Sacred' and 'Secular' music. Popular music, usually accompanied by 'plucked' instruments, took innumerable forms and the most well-known is probably the ballad; the

Frottola, Villotta, Rispetto and *Strambotto*, and the ever present polyphonic songs, which were more 'courtly' in Italy and France and more 'spiritual' in Germany and 'mystical' Spain. One of the most important forms of secular music was the Madrigal.

As far as sacred music was concerned, the common forms were the Motet (a polyphonic form of vocal or instrumental music, which was performed in a liturgical context) and the Mass (a composition with fixed parts of the mass in Latin), with its various specifications; the *Requiem*, the *Missa Solemnis*, the *Missa Brevis*, etc.

The choice of instruments to perform these pieces was established only when they were to be performed, in accordance with the place and the number of instruments available to the musicians.

The musical instruments of the Renaissance, perfected versions of those already used in the Middle Ages, were divided according to the theoretical criteria established many centuries earlier by the late Roman philosopher Boethius (475 - 525 AD), which were; String, Wind and Percussion instruments.

But which were the actual instruments that played the compositions?

To start with, we can make the distinction between String and 'Keyboard' instruments. Among the most widely used are of the first category, which was the *Lira da Braccio*, an instrument whose strings were rubbed, the forerunner of the Violin, which kept the straight peg box of the ancient *Vielle*. It was heart-shaped with pegs and five strings, of which the two lowest were placed outside the neck of the instrument and acted as drones. The other stringed instruments frequently used by the musicians of the period were the Harp, the Guitar, the Lute, the Rebec, the Marine Trumpet (despite its name, it is a fully stringed instrument) and the Vihuela.

Among the keyboard instruments, on the other hand, in addition to the Harpsichord and the Clavichord, the Pipe Organ was hugely important, as the instrument of choice for 'Sacred Music'.

Since 900 AD, the Church had authorized Pipe Organs to be used for the performance of 'Sacred Music' during liturgical celebrations. The Organs of the period were modest in size since in general they had only a limited number of pipes at their disposal. There were two types; Portative and Positive. The first took up little space and often had only one row of pipes and a keyboard with few notes.

It was possible to play them while carrying them slung over one shoulder, with one hand working the bellows and the other using the small keyboard. Since they were easy to handle, they were used for religious processions.

The Positive Organs (which were positioned in a given place) were bigger, had several rows of pipes and a larger keyboard than the portable instruments and their use was confined to the interior of churches. The Positive Organs required the presence of another person to work the bellows, as well as the organist. Both types of organ were initially without pedals, which appeared only around 1400, marking the birth of the 'Great Organ'.

As mentioned earlier, it remained for me to clarify a question that I consider important; whether or not there was a pipe organ in the Dominican church of Santa Maria delle Grazie at the time when *The Last Supper* was being painted. We can make a quick chronology of the history of this beautiful Italian church. Founded in 1463, its design was by the well-known architect, Guiniforte Solari.

The building works started in 1465 and ended in 1482. The original structure of the building was a typical example of Lombard late-Gothic art, of which Solari was a notable exponent. From 1490, Ludovico Sforza had the church undergo substantial architectural modification; he had decided to make it into a Mausoleum for his family. The Moor called in the best artists of the period to achieve his project.

He entrusted Bramante (the Architect) with the creation of the new *Tribune*, he awarded Cristoforo Solari (the Architect and Painter) the covering of the Sepulcher placed in the center of the Choir, while in 1494 Leonardo was commissioned to paint *The Last Supper*. Below, at floor level, a Choir made in wood and a Pipe Organ were placed in the Apse of the church. I found the information I needed to show the presence of the Pipe Organ during the work on *The Last Supper* in a document written by Fra' Girolamo Gattico, whom I have already quoted in a previous chapter:

"A succinct and true description of the things relating to the church and monastery of Santa Maria delle Grazie and Santa Maria della Rosa and its place, and other contacts of theirs in Milan of the order of the Preachers, with two tables at the end."

In the thirteenth chapter, on pages 46 and 47, the friar wrote:

"About the Organ. In view of the great crowd of worshippers going to church every day to worship the picture

of Our Lady of Graces – the miraculous holy picture that every hour bestowed favors, as Fra' Girolamo put it – some benefactors of the Milanese nobility decided to donate a Pipe Organ so that the liturgy could be accompanied by Sacred music. Thus, in 1490, under the priorate of Father Fra' Sebastiano da Brescia, the Organ made by Master Fachetto was installed, with the consent of the Dominican fathers, in the choir of the central nave of the church."

It is certain, therefore, that the Pipe Organ was installed in Santa Maria delle Grazie in 1490, four years before Leonardo began his painting in the refectory. Further confirmation of this concerns the figure of Bartolomeo Antegnati, a well-known builder of Pipe Organs, who, in 1490, was called to Milan for the restoration and partial remaking of the northern Organ of the Cathedral of Milan. The workshop where he carried out his work, was, strangely enough, at Santa Maria delle Grazie.

Antegnati played the Organ in this church on several occasions and precisely at the time when Leonardo was working on his masterpiece.

This information was valuable for my research, because it allowed me to reasonably assume that Leonardo, in the place where he was working, would also have the opportunity to use an Organ in order to compose and play his music. In all probability, he was also able to attend Antegnati's performances, the latter being not only a competent builder and restorer of Organs, but also an excellent Instrumentalist.

There is only one doubt still to be explained; is the "Fachetto" cited both by Fra' Girolamo Gattico and Bartolomeo Antegnati the same person?

The year, 1490, matches perfectly and after all, how many 'famous builders' and 'Organ players' could be called in by a duke in just one year?

IX

In order to transcribe the musical signs on to a score, I decided to use the natural method of Guido d'Arezzo, now commonly called the 'Treble Clef' or the 'Violin Clef', as I had done previously when the only 'notes' I had identified were the bread rolls. So, I started also from the assumption that the first note on the first line, starting low, was a **mi (E)** and that the highest – Thomas's finger – had therefore to be a **fa (F)**.

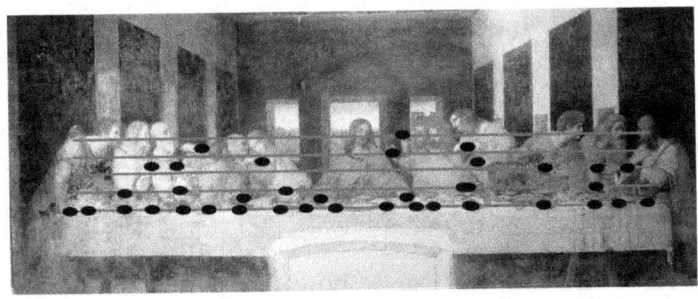

I examined each individual note of the musical outline

with care. Some notes, at first sight, seemed to be parallel with each other, but in reality they could not be played at the same time. In fact, even the smallest, imperceptible difference between one note and another, would ensure that they had to be played separately, otherwise a dissonance would be created.

The musical sequence (reading naturally from the right to the left) started off with a **mi (E)**; the second note was a **ti (B)** (in other words, the seventh of the seven notes); the third note was again a **mi (E)**; the following three notes were aligned with each other. The sequence consisted of a **mi (E)**, a **so (G)** and a **ti (B)**: – a triad (three again...).

In musical theory, a chord is formed of a first note, called the Tonic, a third called the Mode or Mediant, and a fifth called the Dominant. Looking at the three notes I had just transcribed, I was overcome by emotion; a **mi (E)**, a **so (G)** and a **ti (B)**. With the 1st, 3rd and 5th degree of the scale, a perfect **E** minor chord at the beginning of the melody (minor third and perfect fifth, therefore a 'consonant diatonic').

Could this be a coincidence?

I continued feverishly to transcribe notes onto the score. Here was the complete sequence of the music, going from the bread roll cut in half at the right end of the table to the bread held in Bartholomew's hand: **mi (E), ti (B), mi (E),** then a chord **mi (E) / so (G) / ti (B),** then again **ti (B), mi (E), do (C),** another chord **mi (E) / so (G) / octave of mi (E)** (it could not be otherwise, since the octave of **mi (E)** must necessarily be linked to the low **mi (E)** on the first line), **mi (E)** repeated twice (later, from other indications, I would discover that this was a single note), **fa (F)**, in the first space starting from below and another **fa (F)** on the last line. In practice, the basic **fa (F)** and its octave, **re (D), mi (E), mi (E), fa (F), mi (E)**.

At this point in the transcription, the sequence showed a **mi (E)** and a **so (G)**. I had already decided, for reasons I explained earlier, that Judas' left hand was not included in the melody in order not to contaminate its sound. But if his hand were not a note, it must nevertheless be an indication regarding the **mi (E)** and the **so (G)** that were adjacent to it, for example, that they should be linked together.

The notes after Judas' hand were: **do (C), fa (F), mi (E)** and another **mi (E)** with its octave; then another chord, **mi (E) / so (G) / do (C)**, a reversal of the chord of **C** major. Then **mi (E), do (C)** (a bichord), **mi (E), so (G)** (another bichord) and, finally, twice **mi (E)** (but in this case too, subsequent indications led me to play the two **mi (E)** as a single note).

Having finished transcribing the sequence, I put the score onto the piano. I was excited, my hands shook and my heart was beating fast. Was I to hear a piece of music last played by Leonardo five hundred years ago, or would I hear another hotchpotch of unrelated notes?

I slowly brought my hands to the keyboard, almost afraid, and I started to play the sequence. I held my breath while my fingers sought the notes on the keyboard, but I immediately realized that this time what I was playing had a precise melodic sense. I reached the end of the phrase and released all the air from my lungs, realizing that I had been holding my breath since I played the first **mi (E)**.

These notes that were echoing in the room, slow and austere, had just been released from a spell that had lasted five centuries. It was as if a casket that had always been there under everyone's eyes without anyone ever lifting its lid, had suddenly been opened.

But the melody emerging from the black balls that I had superimposed on to the bread rolls and the hands, was unified, without pauses, without time signature, without any sense of rhythm. I think it is easy for my readers – even for those who are not musicians – to imagine that a simple sequence of notes cannot yet be called a 'piece of music', unless we know *how long each note should last.*

I had already hypothesized that the music of *The Last Supper,* needing to emphasize the drama of the moment the fresco represented, could only be dramatic. Now I found myself thinking again of the gesture of the Apostle Andrew, as he seemed to be indicating slower movement. I then tried to play the phrase again (in fact, Andrew came to mind once more after I had already played it a hundred times), slowing the speed of execution to an *adagio*. In fact, this gave me the feeling that I was approaching the composer's intentions, but feelings alone were not enough.

I needed to write some numbers, black on white.

I started by copying out the music onto the score and assigning each note the value of **1/4**, a quarter note or crotchet, given that I had found no indication on the *Holy Table* of notes similar to the eighth note or quaver, which has the value of **1/8**. For this reason, I directed my research toward musical figures that were no shorter than a quarter note. It was a first step, but it did not bring me much closer to solving the basic problem; what value was to be given to each individual note?

In other words, how long did each one last?

In order to explain how I reached a solution, I need to

open a brief parenthesis on musical theory, which could be more difficult to read than what you have read so far, but I will do my best to limit it to what is strictly necessary.

If, as in this case, the time signature for performing a piece is **3/4**, it means that each bar must contain duration values of the notes which, added together, always result in **3/4**. I should have explained that if in the first bar I had to write, for example, three quarter notes (of a value of **1/4** each, then added together, they make **3/4**), or one quarter note (of the value of **1/4**) linked by a tie to a half note, or minim, (a value of **2/4**) added together would still result in the necessary **3/4**.

The tie joins two or more notes of the same level, so that to the value of the first note is added that of the second.

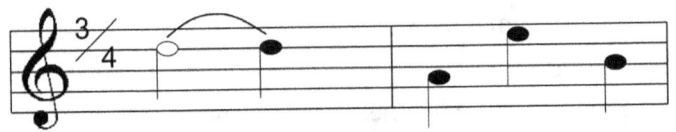

The doubt over the duration of the notes kept me occupied for some time. Then, one day, I remembered the 'movement' I had noticed in the hands of the Apostles on Jesus' left.

The hands of the first three Apostles had a sinuous, soft action, like a wave. Simon's spread hands seemed to touch the right hand of Jude Thaddeus, forming a group of three hands, while the left hand of Matthew, the third Apostle, is further away from the hands of the first two. A similar arrangement can be seen also in the second group of Apostles. In fact, the right hand of Matthew, who forms part of the first group, creates a base for the hands of Philip, the fourth Apostle from the right, creating again a group of three hands.

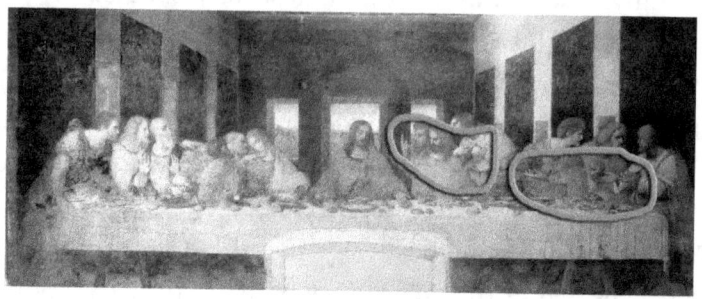

In this case too, the right hand of James the Greater, fifth from the right, is held outwards like that of Matthew. In this way, Leonardo twice created a group of three hands from which one hand keeps its distance. It seemed to me, at a glimpse, that I could see a precise internal rhythmic movement, a recurrent movement, which made the three to one ratio stand out.

Three to one, three to one, three to one.

Thinking about it, there was something in the overall picture which affirmed this relationship, both visually and theologically. Each group of Apostles leans toward and is tied to Jesus, the incarnation of the triune God. **Three to One**.

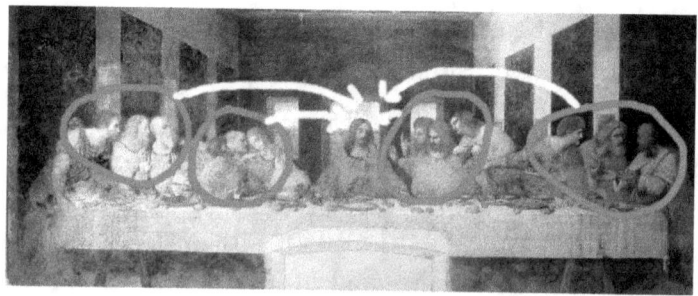

With this, the last, tiny piece of the puzzle fell into place.

By now, I had learned not to overlook any detail of the painting, because everything contributed to forming an organic and harmonious whole, in which each small detail, even the most insignificant, was in reality a precise clue. Furthermore, I had always been certain, from the very beginning of this investigation, that each element of the enigma was expressed in a clear and recognizable way. If I had overlooked anything, sooner or later I would find the element that had escaped.

It was in this way that one day I found myself reflecting on a small piece of fruit, an orange to be precise, which was on the table next to one of the bread rolls, both of them in front of a dish that Leonardo had placed immediately under Matthew's left hand.

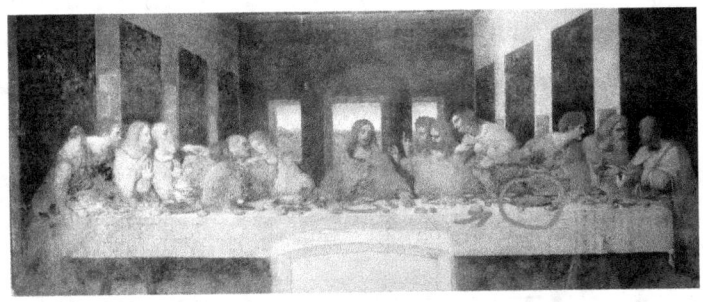

The modest size of the fruit compared to the larger size of the bread rolls probably meant something, I thought. In musical terms, a much smaller notation of a note is called a 'Dot'. The Dot is a graphic sign, which, beside a note, increases the duration of that note by a half. The bread roll, on the other hand, in this musical reading, represents a **2/4** note or a *half note*.

According to the rule I explained above – that the sum of the notes contained within a bar had to match the time signature – if the smallest element (the fruit) was a dot, then with a value of **1/4**, the bread roll matching Matthew's hand must necessarily be a **2/4** note, or a half note, to ensure that the sum of the two values produced a result of **3/4**, in other words, the value required by the time signature.

If the movement of the first three Apostles' hands measured the mathematical value of the first bar (which was **1/4** for each note, that is to say, three quarter notes: a ratio of **(3)**, then the 'fourth hand' of Matthew, isolated and distant from the group of three, defined the metric division of the second bar, thus a long note with the whole value of **3/4**: a ratio of **(1)**.

I amended the mathematical value of the notation, ensuring that the duration of the notes in the first bar were all quarter notes, in other words, **mi (E)** 1/4, **ti (B)** 1/4, **mi (E)** 1/4; while the values of the following bar were represented by three half notes tied to a dot: **mi (E)** 3/4, **so (G)** 3/4, **ti (B)** 3/4.

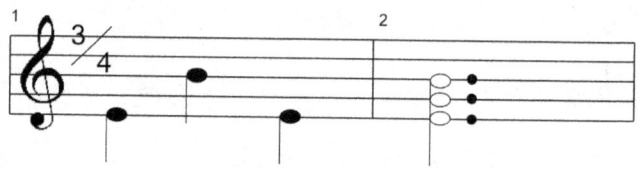

The passage transcribed in this way finally had a precise musical sense.

Everything fitted, and now, the music had its precise structure, a mathematical duration.

The speed of execution, as mentioned earlier, was *adagio* and the piece sounded like a sort of *requiem*. Music that was definitely dramatic, but also dark, solemn, austere. It could not have been otherwise, since it accompanied the moment of Christ's betrayal, the beginning of His Passion.

As we know, Leonardo's mastery in creating complicated gear systems allowed him to contribute to many fields. I discovered that he was very interested in instruments for measuring time.

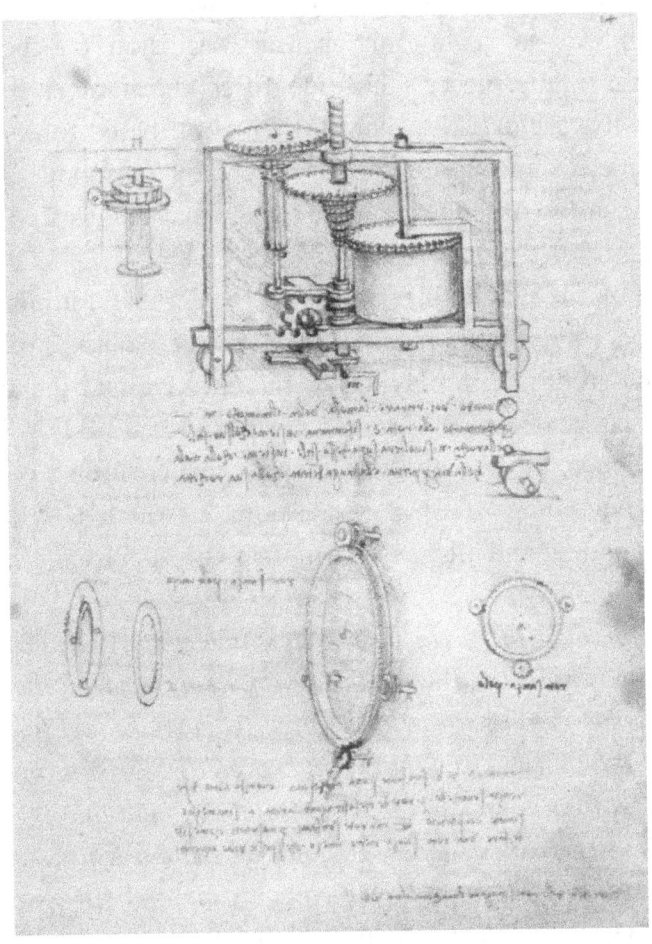

Clock mechanism – Madrid Codex I – National Library of Madrid – sheet 14 recto

His pen brought to life Hourglasses, Sundials and sophisticated mechanisms applicable both to the Clocks of the time or to the 'Automatons' he created.

He drew them to study them and above all, to improve them, so that he could achieve that precision of movement and time that for him was almost a Platonic ideal.

The last part of the research on the music in *The Last Supper* was in reality an arbitrary decision on the total duration of the piece. I had identified the number of bars, thanks to various clues that all then contributed to a sudden theological intuition linked to the episode of the multiplication of the loaves and fishes; that it consisted of the number of the Apostles.

It took me much longer to guess the actual duration of the melody. I played the music, looked at the painting, read the Gospels, returned to playing. In the end, I found the answer in a passage from St. Mark's Gospel (15: 33-37) – by no coincidence, the passage, if the scene in Leonardo's painting is the beginning of Christ's Passion, in which His Passion had its ending and all was accomplished:

"And when the sixth hour was come, there was darkness over the whole land until the ninth hour. And at the ninth hour Jesus cried with a loud voice, saying, Eloi, Eloi, lama sabachthani? which is, being interpreted, My God, my God, why hast thou forsaken me? And some of them that stood by, when they heard [it], said, Behold, he calleth Elias. And one ran and filled a spunge full of vinegar, and put [it] on a reed, and gave him to drink, saying, Let alone; let us see whether Elias will come to take him down. And Jesus cried with a loud voice, and gave up the ghost."

The Passion of Christ took place, therefore, between the sixth and the ninth hour or, in our division of the day, between midday and three in the afternoon.

I tried to multiply the numbers relative to the 'time' of the Passion, that is the sixth hour by the ninth hour: **6 x 9 = 54**. The result had no apparent links with *The Last Supper,* but I wondered whether in Leonardo's mind, the number **54** was linked to a measurement of the duration.

I still remember the moment when, after setting the metronome to **54** as the speed of execution, I timed the duration of the melody: and it was exactly **forty seconds**. This is another highly symbolic value, a further confirmation, at theological level, that the division of the music into 12 bars was correct, as was also the duration of the notes.

The Israelites spent 40 years in the desert and Moses spent 40 days on Mount Sinai. It is quoting these 'purifying' periods that the Gospels tell us about the 40 days Jesus spent alone in the desert, but it is not enough. After the Resurrection, Jesus spent 40 days with the Apostles, before sending them out into the world to proclaim the Good News. Once again, each mathematical reference arising from the painting was linked to the same recurring matrices.

I attempted to divide the duration of the melody by the number of bars; **40/12**. I was amazed; the result was **3.33333** recurring. Once again it was three – repeated to infinity! – once again a reference to the mystery of the *Holy Trinity.*

Could all this be just a coincidence?

Now that I had established all the variables, the musical phrase I played on the piano had overall a precise melodic and harmonic sense and it ended exactly in correspondence with the first Apostle from the left, Bartholomew.

The most extraordinary thing was that the end of the phrase seemed to merge perfectly with the beginning, like a sort of *moto perpetuo*, perpetual motion. Thinking of how many times Leonardo took delight in the elegance and effectiveness of the 'endless lives' of his machines, I could not help but imagine that for *The Last Supper*, he had composed an 'endless music'.

I continued to analyze the melodic/harmonic structure of the piece, seeking its exact tonality.

We have to remember, as mentioned in the chapter on Renaissance music, that the music of the period was modal and not tonal as it later became.

What I found in the musical phrase was one of the authentic modes, specifically the Phrygian, a dark mode, gloomy, little used in modern music, which was formed starting from **mi** (**E**).

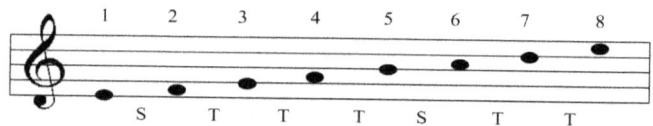

The scale in Phrygian mode corresponds exactly to the natural scale: mi, fa, so, la, ti, do, re, mi, with no alteration. To make a transcription possible in modern style, I had to find the correct tonality.

The first chord formed in the music of *The Last Supper*, was **E** minor, so the tonality of execution had to be in **E** minor.

The following are transcriptions, first in modern key and then in the writing of the period.

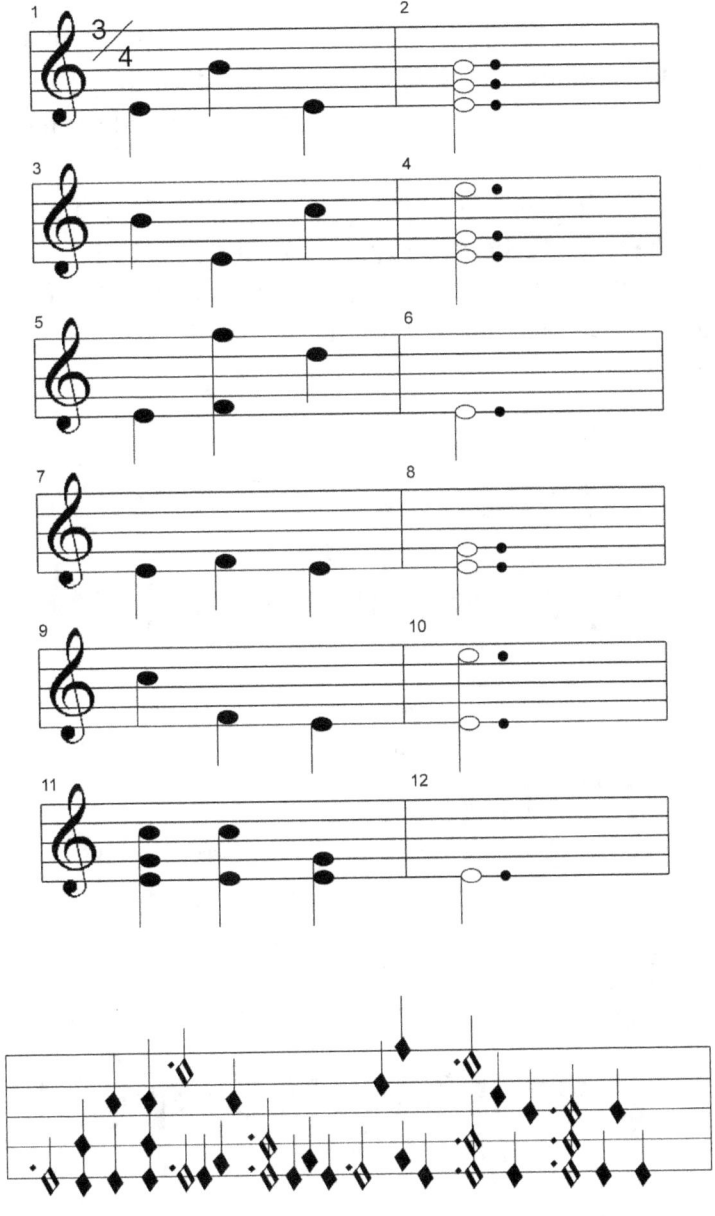

(Attempt at transcription in accordance with the notation system of the period, but to be read from right to left)

At this point and since this was sacred music, I requested authorization to play the musical phrase on the 1867 pipe organ in the convent of San Francesco in Palestrina, near Rome.

It was the most suitable instrument to bring into relief 'The Passion of Christ' piece contained in *The Last Supper*.

I copied the recording on to the computer and using graphic software, developed the finger positions on the keyboard.

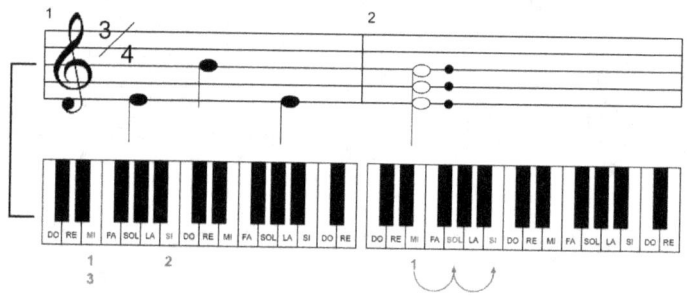

A: First and second measure.
Musical sequenze:
(1) mi (E), ti (B), mi (E);
(2) mi (E) minor chord (mi (E)/so (G)/ ti (B);

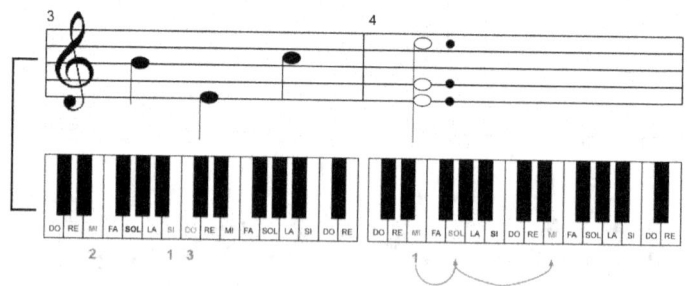

B: Third and fourth measure.
Musical sequenze: *(3)* ti (B), mi (E), do (C);

(4) chord mi (E)/so (G)/octave of mi (E);

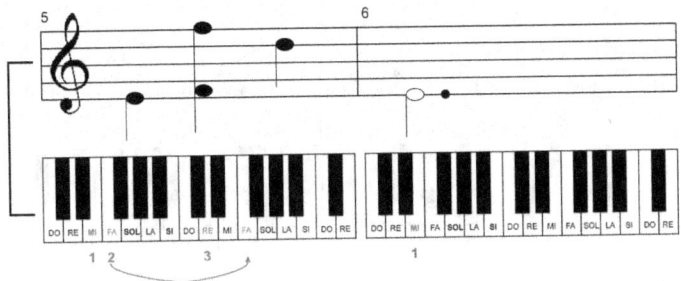

C: Fifth and sixth measure.
  Musical sequence: *(5)* mi (E), fa (F) / fa (F) octave, re (D); *(6)* mi (E);

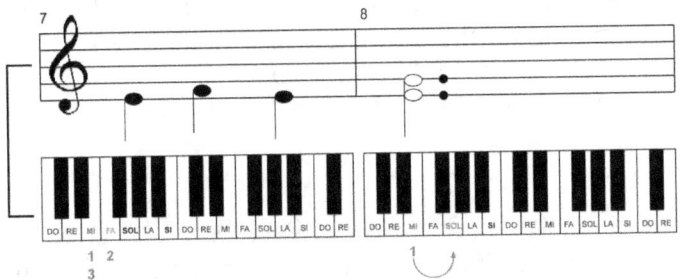

D) Seventh and eighth measure.
  Musical sequenze: *(7)* mi E), fa (F), mi (E); *(8)* bichord mi (E) / so (G);

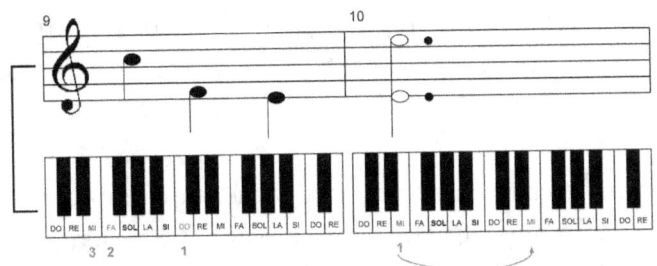

E) Ninth and tenth measure.
  Musical sequenze: *(9)* do (C), fa (F), mi (E);

(10) mi (E)/ octave of mi (E);

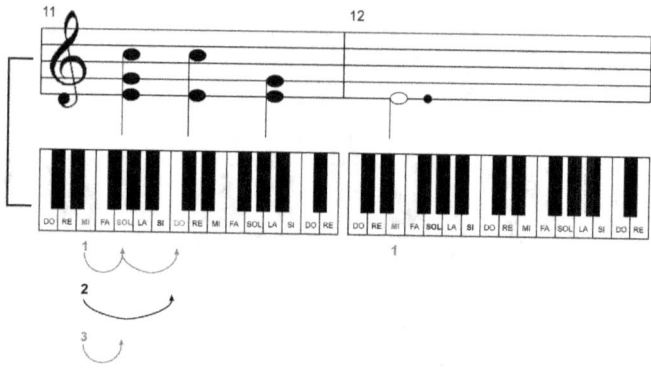

F) Eleventh and twelfth measure.
Musical sequence: *(11)* chord mi (E) / so (G) / do (C) (reversal of the major chord of do (C) − bichord mi (E) / do (C) − bichord mi (E) / so (G);
(12) final mi (E).

It is sufficient to look at the positions on the keyboard to realize the peculiarity of the piece as far as its performance is concerned. the melody was specially written in such a way that it is the left hand that plays the main parts, with the right playing only a few notes. Well, it is a well-known fact that Leonardo was left-handed and proud of it, to the extent of learning to write from right to left. Yet more proof, of my assertion − that this great, left-handed genius was also the composer of this melody?

In order to have a neutral but authoritative opinion of the melodic-harmonic structure of the piece, I decided to submit Leonardo's melody to Father Innocenzo Schipani, Franciscan friar and official organist (as well as director) of the Corale

Polifonica 'Antoniana' at the Basilica of Sant'Antonio in Rome. After listening to the phrase, Father Innocenzo made the following comment:

"From listening to the melody, the impression I have is one of a scale of oriental character in the modal system".

Biography

Giovanni Pala is a Scholar of the most enigmatic works and the most impervious codes of Leonardo da Vinci and he is known worldwide for his research. He has participated in Documentary Productions for the History Channel and has been interviewed by major International Networks, such as; CNN, BBC, Discovery News and NHK.

As a writer, he has published this books: *The Hidden Music: A Mystery Unveiled After Five Hundred Years* (2007) published in Italy, Japan, and Central, and South America; *Leonardo: The Hidden Secret* (2015) translated into English, and sold in the United States; *Leonardo: Il Manoscritto Perduto* (2021), published and sold in Italy; *Leonardo: El Diario Prohibido* (2021), published in United States, Central, and South America.

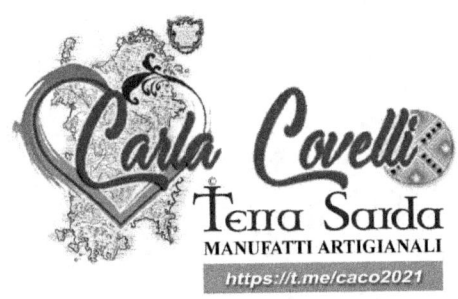

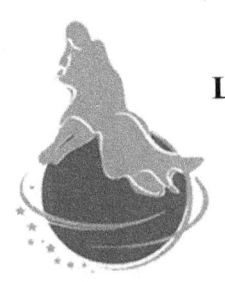

LA DEA MADRE VIAGGI
Il tuo Tour Operator in Sardegna

www.ladeamadreviaggi.com

© December 2020 – **ALIC Publishing House Inc.**

LOS ANGELES – MEXICO CITY – LONDON – MOSCOW – SIDNEY
TOKYO – MADRID

2399 North Sepulveda Blvd.
Los Angeles, California 90077
U.S.A.

www.ingramcontent.com/pod-product-compliance
Lightning Source LLC
Chambersburg PA
CBHW070235220526
45465CB00004B/1428